Everyday Idioms

for Reference and Practice

Book Two

D0060911

Ronald E. Feare

LONGMAN

Everyday Idioms for Reference and Practice: Book Two

Pearson Education, 10 Bank Street, White Plains, NY 10606

Editorial director: Joanne Dresner
Senior acquisitions editor: Allen Ascher
Associate editor: Jessica Miller
Production editor: Christine Cervoni
Text design: Christine Gehring Wolf
Text art: Len Shalansky
Cover design adaptation: Naomi Ganor

Library of Congress Cataloging-in-Publication Data

Feare, Ronald E.
    Everyday idioms for reference and practice / Ronald E. Feare.
      p. cm.
    Includes index.
    ISBN 0-201-83408-1 (v. 1)
    1. English language—Textbooks for foreign speakers. 2. English
language—Idioms.   I. Title.
PE1128.F33   1997
428.2'4—dc20   95-53996
                                    CIP

ISBN: 0-201-44181-0

7 8 9 10 - CRS - 06 05 04 03 02

Contents

iii

Contents

Contents

Contents

Preface

Everyday Idioms for Reference and Practice is a two-level series for intermediate through advanced students. The series is designed to make it easier to learn and master common American idioms.

   Book Two contains almost 600 idiomatic expressions organized thematically into 50 logical, easy-to-access categories including common situations, topics, and functions in English. The idioms within each category share related meaning or purpose. This arrangement makes it easy to successfully find, learn, and remember the idioms.

   The over 1,200 idioms in both books were carefully selected from dozens of popular newspapers and magazines, workbooks and dictionaries on idiomatic expressions, as well as idiom samples collected by students at the American Language Institute, San Diego State University. *Book Two* includes common and useful idioms that will increase **high–intermediate and advanced** students' ability to comprehend and speak English more fluently.

Unit Format

Each unit opens with a list of idioms with definitions and example sentences that provide clear contexts for usage. Parentheses indicate if a part of the idiom is optional. Many entries also provide additional synonymous, antonymous, or related idioms. If appropriate, grammar and usage notes are included.

Grammar and Usage Notes

Grammar notes are provided when necessary to clearly explain how to use an idiom correctly. For example, some verbal idioms may be used with or without an object:

		OBJECT	
They had to	*wake up*	George	before 6:30.
Ginger usually	*wakes up*		before her parents.

Some verbal idioms are separable; that is, an object may separate the parts of the idiom:

	OBJECT	
I won't *clean up*	the bedroom	if you don't help me.
I won't *clean*	the bedroom	*up* if you don't help me.

Sometimes a verbal idiom *must* be separated by an object:

OBJECT

A cup of coffee **gets**   me   **going** in the morning.

Usage notes provide information about level of formality, social use, and collocations.

Exercises

Exercises in each unit offer opportunities to speak, listen, read, and write. They progress from controlled to open-ended and more difficult.

Exercise A asks students to show they recognize each idiom by completing the missing idioms in single sentences, paragraphs, or dialogues. When a verb is the missing part, the tense or third person singular ending -*s* must be written correctly.

Exercise B asks students to show they understand an idiom by matching a question with its appropriate response. To do this as an optional listening exercise, students cover the questions in the left column and the teacher reads the questions aloud.

Exercise C gives students further practice in understanding and using the idioms through pair discussion or writing. Each question uses one or more idioms from the unit.

Exercise D is an open-ended opportunity to practice the idioms through speaking or writing as students role-play, discuss, give an oral presentation, or create a dialogue related to the unit topic.

Review Units

There is a review unit after every ten units. Each review unit provides further practice in using the idioms in multiple-choice exercises, true/false exercises, and crossword puzzles.

It is possible to use a review unit as a pretest to determine how many idioms are really known from the ten preceding units. This may help determine which units should be studied first. If they are not used as pretests, each review unit should be done only after completing the ten units that precede it.

How to Use the Book

This book may be used as a class text, a supplementary text, a self-study text, or as a reference. Though the two *Everyday Idioms* books can be used as a series, it is not necessary to use *Book One* before using *Book Two*. Units can be studied in any order and, by referring to the unit topics, they can be easily used to supplement lessons in speaking or writing. The table of contents lists the categories clearly along with the respective idioms in each unit, making them easily accessible. The index at the back of the book also provides a complete alphabetical listing of the idioms with page number reference. There is a perforated answer key for Exercises A and B and the review units at the back of the book.

Unit 1
Timing

all of a sudden   suddenly, without warning
- Jane was driving on the highway when *all of a sudden* her engine quit.
- The lightning flashed, and *all of a sudden* there was no electricity in the house.

in no time   very quickly, not taking much time
also: **in a flash**
- The excited children got ready for the trip to the zoo *in no time.*
- The small hummingbird slowly flew close to us and then, *In a flash,* it was gone.

not miss a beat   to continue doing something without hesitation
USAGE NOTE: This idiom refers to the ability to continue doing something despite an interruption. Other negative forms such as *without* and *never* can be used instead of *not.*
- Even though angry demonstrators shouted during his speech, the politician did*n't miss a beat.*
- When the teleprompter failed, the TV newscaster kept reporting *without missing a beat.*

right away   immediately
also: **at once**
- I'm going to the store to buy a couple of items and I'll be back *right away.*
- Johnny, go to your room and study *at once!*

as soon as   immediately after
GRAMMAR NOTE: This idiom is a conjunction that combines two sentences into one.
- *As soon as* Helena got home, she checked the mailbox for a letter from her daughter.
- Mark left the boring conference presentation *as soon as* it ended.

in the long run   eventually, in the future
also: **in the end**
- If you work hard and do your best, *in the long run* you will succeed.
- Even though the Madisons almost got divorced, they managed to reconcile *in the end.*

so far   from the past to the present, until now
> also: **to this day**

- Angie entered the writing contest three months ago, but *so far* she hasn't heard anything.
- Mohammed never explained why he quit his job, and *to this day* we still don't know why.

be (just) about to   to be at the moment of doing something

GRAMMAR NOTE: The idiom itself is followed by the base form of a verb, even though a gerund (verb + *-ing*) is used in the definition.

- Mr. Ochoa *was about to* play golf when it started to rain.
- Oh, hi, Marta. I'm glad you called me. I *was just about to* leave for the beach.

at the last minute   at the last possible moment

USAGE NOTE: This idiom is used when someone is almost too late to do something or to be somewhere.

- Minu was planning to go with us but changed his mind *at the last minute.*
- *At the last minute* the manager had to cancel the meeting because of illness.

EXERCISES

A.   Fill in each blank with the appropriate form of an idiom from this unit. Some sentences may have more than one correct answer.

1. _____ _____ _____ I receive the information you've requested, I'll call you.

2. It's impossible to delay this project even one week. It must be completed _____ _____.

3. The amateur pianist surprised even herself by performing all the selections well. She didn't _____ _____ _____ at all.

4. Why is it so difficult for me to accomplish things in a timely fashion? I always seem to be doing them _____ _____ _____ _____.

5. Oh, hi, there, Mac. I _____ _____ _____ _____ leave when I heard the phone ring.

6. Debbie hasn't been able to do all the homework exercises. _____ _____ she has completed only five out of eight problems.

7. The sky grew darker, the wind became stronger, and _____ _____ _____ _____ it began to rain.

8. You may not enjoy exercising right now, but you'll appreciate the results _____ _____ _____ _____.

9. It takes Martha only twenty minutes to get ready for work in the morning. It's amazing how she's out the door _____ _____ _____.

B. Choose the statement in the right column that best responds to each question in the left column. Write the appropriate number in the blank.

1. Will you remember to call me about the package as soon as it arrives?

2. When you got the flu all of a sudden, did you have to miss work?

3. Is the report going to be done at the last minute again, Tom?

4. What were you just about to tell me?

5. How have you benefited from your exercise program so far?

____ a. No, I was able to keep working without missing a beat.

____ b. I can't remember. To this day I have a poor memory.

____ c. Yes, I'll be sure to contact you about it right away.

____ d. No, in fact, it'll be ready in no time. You'll have it tomorrow.

____ e. I feel good, and in the long run I'll feel even better.

C. Use the idioms in your spoken or written answers to the following questions.

1. What would you probably do *right away* after learning that a big hurricane or typhoon was headed toward your area?

2. What important things have you accomplished in your life *so far?*

3. What is the single most important thing you'd like to accomplish *in the long run?*

4. Have you ever *been just about to* go to sleep and been interrupted? Who interrupted you? What did you do?

5. What kind of unpleasant task would you tend to do *at the last minute?*

D. Using the idioms from this unit, develop a presentation about a real or imaginary day when you were very busy. Talk about what you did and when you did it. You may want to include the following information:

- how fast you did things;
- the order in which you did them;
- if you were doing something and were interrupted;
- if something happened suddenly.

Unit 2
Number and Quantity

at least   at the minimum, no fewer than
   opposite meaning: **at most** (at the maximum, no more than)
   GRAMMAR NOTE: This idiom precedes a number modifying a noun, or follows the noun itself.

   ■ *At least* 50,000 people attended the rock concert in the stadium.
   ■ That jacket selling for one hundred dollars costs thirty dollars *at most* to manufacture.

be left   to remain
   GRAMMAR/USAGE NOTES: This verbal idiom is always used in the passive form. It is used to refer to quantities and periods of time.

   ■ Only two eggs *are left* in the refrigerator. It's time to buy some more.
   ■ How much time *is left* before the plane is scheduled to depart?

or so   approximately, about
   USAGE NOTE: This idiom follows either a number modifying a noun or the noun itself.

   ■ Lynn was disappointed when only ten *or so* people came to her birthday party.
   ■ Could I borrow twenty dollars *or so* until next week?

a drop in the bucket   a small or insignificant amount or expense
   ■ For a millionaire, the cost of a luxury car is *a drop in the bucket.*
   ■ Incredibly, there were only two inches of snow this year, which was *a drop in the bucket* compared with the usual twenty-five inches.

a number of   some, several
   related idiom: **a lot of** (many, much)
   GRAMMAR NOTES: Even though these idioms include the nouns *number* and *lot*, they function as adjectives that modify nouns. *A number of* always precedes a plural noun, and *a lot of* precedes either a singular or plural noun.

   ■ *A number of* questions regarding company performance were raised at the stockholder's meeting.
   ■ I don't have *a lot of* time to talk right now, even though there are *a lot of* things we have to talk about.

the lion's share   the majority of, most
- *The lion's share* of federal taxes in the United States goes into entitlement programs such as Social Security and Medicare.
- Billy shared some of his candy with his friends, but he kept *the lion's share* for himself.

all told   altogether, in sum

GRAMMAR NOTE: This idiom is usually placed at the beginning of a sentence.
- *All told*, there are twelve separate departments within the university.
- *All told*, the committee was able to raise over $5,000 for the charity fund.

pile up   to remain unaccomplished, to accumulate

USAGE NOTE: This idiom is used for chores or other work that is not done according to normal routine.
- The more I delay in doing household chores, the more they *pile up.*
- When Betty returned to the office from vacation, a lot of mail had *piled up* on her desk.

come up short   to have less than the correct amount

USAGE NOTES: This idiom usually refers to money. The actual amount of money can be added between *up* and *short*.
- Darrin *came up short* when he counted the change that the clerk had given him.
- When the bank teller counted the money in her drawer, she *came up* ten dollars *short.*

EXERCISES

A.   **Fill in each blank with the appropriate form of an idiom from this unit. Some sentences may have more than one correct answer.**

1. The five volunteers were each able to secure about $500 in charitable pledges, so _____ _____ they collected around $2,500.

2. I couldn't believe how much work _____ _____ on my desk while I was away on a business trip!

3. It will take me _____ _____ two weeks, probably three, to do all the work.

4. The district attorney found _____ _____ _____ inconsistencies in the witness's statement, so she decided to file formal charges.

5. The elderly couple's adopted son received _____ _____ _____ of the estate, while two nephews received smaller portions.

6. The couple's estate, the exact value of which won't be known until later, is presently valued at $3 million _____ _____.

7. When the cashier counted the money in her drawer, she was surprised to _____ _____ _____ by about five dollars.

8. A two-dollar contribution to the office coffee fund each month is _____ _____ _____ _____ _____ compared to buying coffee from a vending machine.

9. Could you inform me when only five minutes _____ _____ in the test period?

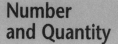

B. Choose the statement in the right column that best responds to each question in the
left column. Write the appropriate number in the blank.

1. How many dirty articles of
clothing are piled up in the
laundry basket?

2. How much money is left in our
bank account?

3. Did a lot of people come to the
wedding reception?

4. Does anyone have two dollars to
cover the rest of our food bill?

5. Did the children divide the cake
among themselves equally?

_____ a. All told, about fifty people attended
the affair.

_____ b. I'd say that there are at least ten
shirts and pants in it.

_____ c. There's a hundred dollars or so in
checking.

_____ d. No, the birthday girl got the lion's
share.

_____ e. I do. That's a drop in the bucket
compared to the total cost!

C. Use the idioms in your spoken or written answers to the following questions.

1. Did you *do a number of* things during your last vacation? What? *All told,* how many
days were you gone?

2. How many months *are left* until your next birthday? *At least* how many years do
you hope to live? How many years *at most?*

3. Do you have any chores or tasks at home or work that are *piling up?* If so, what?

4. Which countries have *the lion's share* of natural resources and wealth in the world?
Is this fair? Why or why not?

5. If you were a millionaire, what kinds of expenses would you consider *a drop in the
bucket?*

D. Using the idioms from this unit or a previous one, tell a classmate about your family.
You may want to include the following:

- how many immediate family members you have;
- whether any of your brothers and sisters remain at home with your parents;
- how housework is accomplished, and who does most of it;
- how many relatives you have in your extended family;
- the minimum number of times each year that your extended family gets together.

Unit 3
Producing and Using

bring out to introduce to the public

GRAMMAR/USAGE NOTES: *Bring out* is separable. It is used when a new version or model of a product is produced.

- The automobile company decided to ***bring*** its new models ***out*** a month earlier than usual.
- Designers from all over the country ***brought out*** their new lines of clothing at the New York fashion show.

turn out to produce (usually in large quantities)

Grammar Note: *Turn out* is separable.

- The modern manufacturing plant ***turns out*** 200 personal computers a day.
- Our new duplicating machine ***turns*** more than forty copies ***out*** per minute.

crank out to produce quickly and in large numbers

also: **whip out**

GRAMMAR/USAGE NOTES: These idioms are separable. They are often used when speed of production is important.

- The software company ***cranked out*** thousands of copies of its new multimedia title in order to meet demand.
- Jake is an amazingly fast writer. He ***whips*** a novel ***out*** each year.

make to order to make to exact specifications, to be custom-made

GRAMMAR NOTES: A noun can separate *make* and *to order*. The idiom can also be used in the passive form.

- The company president has a local tailor ***make*** all her suits ***to order.***
- The Garcias' kitchen cabinets were ***made to order*** by an expert carpenter.

cut down (on) to reduce, to decrease one's use of

also: **cut back (on), cutback** (noun)

GRAMMAR/USAGE NOTES: The use of *on* is optional in some cases. These idioms are usually used in reference to money or bad habits.

- The doctor told Melanie to ***cut down on*** cigarettes if she wanted to avoid lung disease.
- In order to maintain a profitable status, the company ***cut back on*** expenses.
- Government ***cutbacks*** required the elimination of two public agencies.

run out (of)   not to have any more
related idiom: **run low (on)** (not to have much more)

- I've **run out of** ideas for a good science project. Do you have any suggestions?
- We're **running low on** gas. We've got to stop at a service station before we **run out.**

go through   to consume or use all or part of something
also: **use up**
GRAMMAR NOTE: *Use up* is separable.

- With three boys, the Kim family **goes through** a gallon of milk each day.
- I can't find the adhesive tape. Did you **use** it all **up?**

collect dust   to remain unused (usually in storage)

- I wish we hadn't bought that pool table. It's just **collecting dust** in the storage room.
- René rarely drives his two classic automobiles. They just sit in his garage **collecting dust.**

pack rat   someone who keeps almost any item (even useless ones)

- Aunt May is such a **pack rat.** Her closets are all filled with old junk.
- I used to be a **pack rat,** but now I regularly have yard sales to get rid of unnecessary things.

EXERCISES

A.   Fill in each blank with the appropriate form of an idiom from this unit. Some sentences may have more than one correct answer.

1. We should have a yard sale soon so that we can get rid of the stuff that is _____ _____ in the garage.

2. That new manufacturing plant can _____ _____ only two large commercial airplanes each month.

3. That productive songwriter has _____ _____ over thirty songs this year, and four have become big hits.

4. The reason Ms. Nielsen's suits look so nice is that they're _____ _____ _____ by an experienced seamstress.

5. If you want to lose weight, you'll have to _____ _____ _____ fatty foods.

6. Mr. Thomas should stop being a _____ _____ and sell some of his many possessions.

7. The Andersons were a little scared when they _____ _____ _____ gas and were stranded on an isolated country road.

8. Each year the book company _____ _____ its new line of children's books just before the fall buying season.

9. Did you really _____ _____ the whole bag of potato chips by yourself?

B. Choose the statement in the right column that best responds to each question in the left column. Write the appropriate number in the blank.

1. Did you just use up all the orange juice in the refrigerator?

2. Has the city park service run out of operating funds yet?

3. Your new dress is beautiful. Is it made to order?

4. Why do you say that Bernard is a pack rat?

5. When will your company bring out its new line of sunglasses?

____ a. Not yet, but the effects of city cutbacks will be felt soon.

____ b. As soon as the new plant can turn out sufficient quantities.

____ c. Are you kidding? I'm sure it was cranked out in a factory!

____ d. No, but we're definitely running low.

____ e. Because so many things are collecting dust in his house.

C. Use the idioms in your spoken or written answers to the following questions.

1. Have you ever been driving and **run out of gas?** When? What did you do?

2. What kinds of food do you and your family **go through** quickly?

3. Are you a **pack rat?** Do you know someone who is? What does your home or their home look like?

4. Do you pay attention to the new clothing fashions that are **brought out** each year? Why or why not?

5. Are any of your clothes **made to order?** Do you know anyone who has clothes **made to order?**

D. Using the idioms from this unit or a previous one, tell a classmate about the things you have and do in your home or office. You may want to include the following:

- items you use up quickly;
- food you eat but shouldn't;
- things you make or have made;
- old items you never use.

Unit 4
Speed and Pacing

in a hurry   hurried, rushed
    also: **in a rush**

    Usage Note: The adjective *big* can precede the nouns *hurry* and *rush,* or the adverb *such* can precede the article *a.*
- Mr. Lewis was *in a* big *hurry* to get to the bank before it closed.
- Why do you have to leave *in* such *a rush?* Please stay and visit a while longer.

hurry up   to go or do more quickly
    also: **step on it, shake a leg**

    Grammar Note: These idioms are often used in command form.
- We're going to be late for the show. *Hurry up!*
- Leanne had to *step on it* in order to get to her appointment on time.
- Our guests are going to arrive soon, and the house isn't ready yet. *Shake a leg!*

on the double   very quickly
- The soldiers were ordered to get to the general's house *on the double.*
- If we don't leave *on the double,* we'll miss the start of the soccer game.

slow down   to go or do more slowly
    also: **slow up**

    Grammar Note: *Slow down* is used with or without an object, and is separable.
- There's no reason to eat your dinner so quickly. Please *slow* it *down.*
- The speed limit here is 65 miles per hour. Please *slow up!*
- I can't understand what you're saying. Could you *slow down* a bit?

inch along   to move very slowly
    Usage Note: This idiom is used when faster movement is not possible.
- The fireman *inched along* the narrow ledge outside the tenth floor window to rescue the cat.
- During morning and evening rush hours, traffic *inches along* urban highways.

at a snail's pace   very slowly
- If you walk *at a snail's pace,* we'll never get there on time!
- The line in front of the university admissions office moved *at a snail's pace.*

pick up   to increase speed or effort

GRAMMAR/USAGE NOTES: This idiom is often followed by the nouns *speed* or *the pace*, but no object is required.

- Traffic had to slow down through the construction zone, but then it *picked up* speed quickly.
- We're never going to finish the yard work by dark. Let's *pick up* the pace.
- Retail sales *picked up* greatly during the holiday season.

EXERCISES

A.   Fill in each blank with the appropriate form of an idiom from this unit. Some sentences may have more than one correct answer.

Yesterday morning my roommate, Frank, and I woke up an hour late and were _____ _____ big _____ to get to class. I was getting ready quickly, but it seemed that Frank was moving _____ _____ _____ _____. I reminded him of the time and told him to _____ ____ and get ready. We grabbed a couple of doughnuts and flew out the door _____ _____ _____.

We were _____ _____ a little by the traffic on the city streets, but it was a different story on the expressway. Traffic was _____ _____ at about five miles an hour. When we got past the scene of an accident, the traffic gradually _____ _____ speed. Fortunately, we were only ten minutes late to class.

B.   Choose the statement in the right column that best responds to each question in the left column. Write the appropriate number in the blank.

1. Why are you driving along at a snail's pace?
2. Don't we have to pick up the pace if we want to finish this yard work by dark?
3. Why was Mother in a hurry to leave for work this morning?
4. You're speaking too quickly. Could you slow down?
5. Why is the office assistant in such a rush this afternoon?

____ a. Because a phone call slowed her up while she was getting ready.

____ b. Can't you see? The traffic is just inching along.

____ c. Yes, we'll have to shake a leg to get it all done.

____ d. He has to get a package to the post office on the double.

____ e. Oh, I'm sorry. I always hurry up when I'm nervous.

C.   Use the idioms in your spoken or written answers to the following questions.

1. What jobs require people to do things *on the double?* Would you like such a job? Why or why not?

2. What food might you consume *at a snail's pace?*

3. When was the last time you were in traffic that was *inching along?* What was the cause?

4. Is there anyone that you constantly have to tell to *hurry up?* Who is that person?

5. For what sports or hobbies might you hope that the wind would *pick up?*

D.   Using the idioms from this unit or a previous one, develop a dialogue or role play in which two people are driving in traffic when they are late. You may want to include the following:

- where they are going;
- what caused them to be late;
- whether one person is telling the other person how he or she should drive;
- how fast or slow traffic is moving.

Unit 5
Patience and Nervousness

hold one's horses   to be patient

    also: **keep one's shirt on**

    GRAMMAR NOTE: These idioms are often used in command form.

    ▪ *Hold your horses!* I'm not ready to go yet.

    ▪ Ernie was so eager to ride the rollercoaster that his dad had to tell him to *keep his shirt on.*

take one's own sweet time   to do at one's own pace

    also: **drag one's heels**

    GRAMMAR/USAGE NOTES: These idioms are used when someone acts slowly even though others expect faster action. A gerund (verb + *-ing*) phrase usually follows the idiom. The possessive adjective *one's* changes form to agree with the subject.

    ▪ The shopper stood impatiently at the counter while the clerk *took his own sweet time* counting the money.

    ▪ My children always *drag their heels* getting ready for bed at night.

sit tight   to wait patiently to see how a situation will develop

    USAGE NOTE: This idiom is used when it is advisable to see how a situation develops rather than act too early.

    ▪ The board of directors voted to *sit tight* until it was known what a major competitor's next move was.

    ▪ The hikers *sat tight* in a mountaintop cave while a strong storm swept through the area.

try someone's patience   to cause someone to become impatient

    GRAMMAR/USAGE NOTES: This idiom is used when someone repeatedly acts or speaks in a way that causes someone else to become impatient, or when an unpleasant situation continues for too long. In conversation, a continuous verb form is usually used.

    ▪ You should think carefully before you speak. Your constant questions are *trying my patience.*

    ▪ Commuting in heavy traffic every day can *try your patience,* especially when you need to hurry.

jump the gun   to move or act impatiently before the correct or proper time

GRAMMAR NOTE: This idiom is usually followed by a time clause starting with *when.*

- The electronics company *jumped the gun* when it announced a new product several months before it was ready for sale.
- The politician *jumped the gun* when she claimed victory before all the election ballots were counted.

on edge   nervous, anxious

related idiom: **ill at ease** (nervously uncomfortable)

- Elaine's parents were *on edge* the whole time she was traveling through Europe with a friend.
- I felt quite *ill at ease* at the party last night because I didn't know anyone there.

on pins and needles   anxious with anticipation

USAGE NOTE: This idiom is often used with the verb *wait.*

- Temur's friends waited *on pins and needles* for him to appear at the surprise birthday party.
- The children were *on pins and needles* waiting for Christmas Day to arrive.

be wound up   to be tense, to be nervous

USAGE NOTE: Other verbs such as *feel* and *seem,* as well as adverbs such as *all* and *so,* are often used.

- Kevin *was* all *wound up* before his important acting audition.
- Why do you *seem* so *wound up?* Sit back and relax a bit.

EXERCISES

A.   **Fill in each blank with the appropriate form of an idiom from this unit.**

1. I shouldn't have drunk so much coffee. I _____ all _____ _____ from the caffeine.

2. Greg got annoyed as an old lady _____ _____ _____ _____ _____ getting into her car and backing out of the only parking space in the lot.

3. Why do you keep rushing me? _____ _____ _____!

4. When the noise from the apartment next to mine grew louder, it really began to _____ _____ _____.

5. The Carlsons waited _____ _____ _____ _____ to hear whether their daughter had had a baby boy or girl.

6. Out of gas on a lonely desert road, we had no choice but to _____ _____ in our car until help arrived.

7. The lawyer _____ _____ _____ by announcing new evidence to the media before it was presented in court.

8. The mother was _____ _____ about letting her son play by himself down by the lake.

B. Choose the statement in the right column that best responds to each question in the left column. Write the appropriate number in the blank.

1. Do you feel ill at ease about seeing your parents again?

2. Did you take my advice and sit tight on the salary issue?

3. Why is Andy dragging his heels getting ready for his piano recital?

4. Are you on pins and needles waiting for your grade report to arrive?

5. Why do you always take your own sweet time getting ready to leave?

____ a. And why can't you keep your shirt on while I do?

____ b. A little bit. They really tried my patience the last time we were together.

____ c. No, I jumped the gun by talking directly to the payroll clerk.

____ d. He's probably all wound up about performing in public.

____ e. Yes, I'll be on edge until I see what my average is.

C. Use the idioms in your spoken or written answers to the following questions.

1. When would you tell another person to *hold their horses?*

2. What could someone else do that would *try your patience?*

3. What do you do to relax when you *are* all *wound up?* Do you often feel *on edge?* Why or why not?

4. Do you ever *take your own sweet time* to accomplish tasks? When are you most likely to do this?

5. When have you felt *on pins and needles?* Have you ever *jumped the gun* in such a situation? What happened?

D. Using the idioms from this unit or a previous one, develop a presentation about a time when you were impatient with another person. You may want to include the following:

- what the person did to make you feel impatient;
- whether the other person often made you feel this way;
- how you reacted to the situation;
- how the other person felt about your reaction.

Unit 6
Mistakes and Confusion

goof up   to make a mistake
> also: **slip up**

> GRAMMAR/USAGE NOTES: These idioms generally refer to mistakes that result from carelessness or lack of attention. They sometimes occur in question form, even though they are not really questions.

> ▪ The assistant *goofed up* badly when he forgot to order more office supplies.

> ▪ Marcia accidentally put two letters to her closest friends in the wrong envelopes. Did she really *slip up!*

mess up   to do something poorly

> GRAMMAR NOTES: This idiom may be used with or without an object. When an object is used, the idiom is separable.

> ▪ Antonio *messed up* on the test because he hadn't studied enough.

> ▪ I tried to fix the old chair by myself but just managed to *mess* it *up* further.

do over   to do again in order to correct a mistake

> GRAMMAR/USAGE NOTES: An object always separates this idiom. The adverb *again* can be used even though it unnecessarily repeats the meaning.

> ▪ Ms. Lee was unhappy with the paint job on her car, so she told the shop to *do* the work *over.*

> ▪ You've made too many errors on these math problems. Please *do* them *over* again at home.

put one's foot in one's mouth   to say something that one shouldn't have said

> ▪ Soros *put his foot in his mouth* when he made a comment about his boss's weight problem at the office party.

> ▪ When Nancy called her boyfriend by her previous boyfriend's name, she really *put her foot in her mouth!*

slip of the tongue   an accidental comment, an unintended remark

> USAGE NOTES: This idiom is used when someone says something and immediately regrets it. The verb *make* is often used.

> ▪ William made a *slip of the tongue* when he mentioned the surprise farewell party to the person who was retiring.

> ▪ The supervisor immediately regretted talking about the possibility of employee layoffs. What a *slip of the tongue!*

be on the wrong track   to pursue the wrong solution to a problem
opposite meaning: **be on the right track**
related idiom: **bark up the wrong tree** (to be mistaken in thought or action)

- The plumber thought he knew the cause of the flooding, but he *was on the wrong track.*
- The police *were on the right track* in locating the stolen merchandise.
- You're *barking up the wrong tree* if you think I'm responsible for that mistake.

not think straight   to be unable to think clearly
Usage Note: *Hardly* can be used instead of *not.*

- I ca*n't think straight* when there's so much noise in the room. Could you please be quiet?
- I'm so tired that I can *hardly think straight.* I need to get some rest.

mix up   to confuse, to bewilder
related form: **mix-up** (noun)
GRAMMAR NOTES: The active form of *mix up* is separable. In the passive form, it is often used with *get.*

- Your explanation doesn't clarify the situation for me. In fact, it's just *mixing* me *up* further!
- I got *mixed up* at the intersection of three major highways and drove the wrong way.
- There was a *mix-up* in the special order, so the wrong products were delivered.

get our/your/their wires crossed   to miscommunicate with someone
also: **get our/your/their signals crossed**
GRAMMAR/USAGE NOTES: These idioms are used when there is a misunderstanding between two or more persons about the details of an activity. The possessive adjective is always plural.

- Van thought that we were supposed to meet on Wednesday, but I thought it was Thursday. I guess we *got our wires crossed.*
- Jerry blames Miyoko for the fact they *got their signals crossed* about the time of the luncheon.

EXERCISES

A.   Fill in each blank with the appropriate form of an idiom from this unit. Some sentences may have more than one correct answer.

JILL: Hi, Bob. What are you doing?

BOB: Hi, Jill. I have to _____ my math homework _____ again.
                                              1

JILL: Oh, really? Did you _____ _____ badly?
                                            2

BOB: I'll say. I _____ _____ on the majority of the problems.
                          3

JILL: Didn't the teacher explain what to do?

BOB: Yes, but the more she explained, the more I got _____ _____. I'm so
                                                                          4

        confused now that I can't _____ _____ .
                                              5

JILL: That's too bad. You should complain to the teacher about the difficulty of the work.

BOB: I'm afraid that if I complained, I might _____ _____ _____
                                                                  6

        _____ _____ _____!

(continued on next page)

JILL: How?

BOB: She might think that I was blaming her.

JILL: Did other students in the class have a difficult time?

BOB: Yes, and many others had to redo their homework too.

JILL: Then you aren't _____ _____ _____ _____ to blame the teacher
                                       7
for a bad explanation!

BOB: Maybe. I just don't want to make a _____ _____ _____ _____
                                       8
and get into further trouble.

JILL: I see. Say, why didn't you come to the party last Saturday?

BOB: I wanted to. I was going to come with Jack, but he and I _____ _____
                                                           9
_____ _____ about the date. I thought that it was next weekend.

JILL: I bet you got confused because you were struggling with this math.

BOB: No, but that would be a good excuse!

B. Choose the statement in the right column that best responds to each question in the left column. Write the appropriate number in the blank.

1. Was it a slip of the tongue when you called her "Karla" instead of "Carol"?
2. Did you mess up on your science experiment?
3. Aren't you barking up the wrong tree by accusing Maria of lying?
4. Are we finally on the right track with this assignment?
5. Did we get our wires crossed about the best time to meet?

____ a. Not at all. I think she's hiding the fact that she goofed up.
____ b. Yes, I got the wrong results. Now I have to do it over.
____ c. We must have. I'm sorry for the mix-up.
____ d. Yes, it was. I really put my foot in my mouth!
____ e. I don't know. We've been working on it so long that I can't think straight.

C. Use the idioms in your spoken or written answers to the following questions.

1. Have you ever made *a slip of the tongue?* What was it? What could you do to prevent this from happening?
2. What might cause you and a friend to *get your wires crossed?*
3. For what reasons might you *not be able to think straight?*
4. Do you readily admit your mistakes when you *goof up?* Why or why not? What about other people you know?
5. How might the police know if they *are on the right track* in a criminal case?

D. Using the idioms from this unit or a previous one, tell a classmate about a time when you made a serious mistake. You may want to include the following:

- what mistake you made;
- what caused you to make the mistake;
- what you had to do to correct the mistake;
- how you felt during this time.

Unit 7
Plans and Arrangements

cook up   to invent, to create a plan

> GRAMMAR/USAGE NOTES: *Cook up* is separable and is usually used for a clever plan that works in someone's favor but may be unfair to others.

- The businessman *cooked up* a scheme to reduce his tax burden by more than 50 percent.
- You've suggested a perfect solution to our dilemma. How did you *cook* it *up* by yourself?

draw up   to compose or create in a more formal way

> GRAMMAR/USAGE NOTES: This idiom is separable but usually is not separated. It is used for more formal plans and documents.

- The law office helped to *draw up* a formal contract for both parties to sign.
- The neighborhood committee *drew* a plan *up* to fight crime in the area.

map out   to set or establish a plan for
also: **chart out**

> GRAMMAR/USAGE NOTES: These idioms are separable. They are used when detailed plans are made.

- Mary is a very thorough person. She has *mapped out* every step of her education in great detail.
- The Boyds *charted out* their activities for each day of their trip to Africa.

be in the works   to be planned, to be in process
also: **be in store**

> GRAMMAR NOTE: The verb *have* can also be used.

- The software company announced that a major upgrade of its best-selling program *was in the works.*
- The special news show talked about some of the technological changes that *are in store* for us in the coming decade.
- What do you *have in store* for us when we come to Boston to visit you?

on the spur of the moment   spontaneously, without previous planning

- *On the spur of the moment,* Jeff and Ursula decided to eat out instead of cooking dinner.
- Laila almost never maps things out. She prefers to do things *on the spur of the moment.*

play it by ear   to adjust plans as events develop

USAGE NOTE: This idiom is used when it is not possible to plan in advance, or when someone prefers to make decisions as the situation progresses.

- I have no idea what we're going to do once we get to Los Angeles. Let's just *play it by ear.*
- When the videotape failed at the beginning of the training session, the presenter was forced to *play* the rest of *it by ear.*

be up in the air   to be undecided

USAGE NOTE: The adverb *still* is often used.

- The time for the meeting *is* still *up in the air.* Melinda will contact us as soon as the time is established.
- Arrangements for Don and Lisa's wedding *were up in the air* for a long time.

rule out   to refuse to accept something as a choice, to preclude

GRAMMAR NOTE: This idiom is separable.

- The president *ruled* military force *out* as an option during the international crisis.
- The club committee *ruled out* the suggestion that membership dues be raised.

EXERCISES

A.   Fill in each blank with the appropriate form of an idiom from this unit. Some sentences may have more than one correct answer.

1. The Andersons don't like to plan a vacation in advance. They prefer to _____ _____ _____ _____.

2. The Garcias, however, always use guidebooks to _____ _____ every step of their vacation.

3. Yolanda was planning to stay home and go to bed early, but _____ _____ _____ _____ _____ _____ she went out to a movie.

4. The company has been very secretive about its research, so an exciting new product probably _____ _____ _____ _____.

5. The divorce lawyers met to _____ _____ a formal agreement that both sides could sign.

6. What a clever plan you have _____ _____ for circumventing your boss's desires and getting it done your way.

7. The teachers' committee has agreed to arrange demonstrations and push for salary negotiations, but for now it has _____ _____ a strike.

8. The Hammonds wish that they could set a final date for their son's wedding, but unfortunately everything _____ still _____ _____ _____ _____.

B. Choose the statement in the right column that best responds to each question in the left column. Write the appropriate number in the blank.

1. Have you mapped out each day of your trip to South America?

2. Is the location of the picnic still up in the air?

3. When will we be ready to draw up the final contract agreement?

4. What kind of surprise birthday party have you cooked up for Stan?

5. Is an increase in club dues in store for members?

____ a. No, we're going to play it by ear when we travel this time.

____ b. No, raising dues has already been ruled out.

____ c. Yes, we'll decide where to have it on the spur of the moment.

____ d. I have something special in the works. He's going to love it.

____ e. First we've got to chart out the details more clearly.

C. Use the idioms in your spoken or written answers to the following questions.

1. Do you *map out* a trip in advance, or do you prefer to *play it by ear?* What are the advantages and disadvantages of each approach?

2. What kinds of activities do you like to do *on the spur of the moment?*

3. What kinds of documents might you have *drawn up* by a lawyer?

4. For what reasons might plans for an activity with your friends *be up in the air?*

5. Are there any jobs that you would *rule out* as career choices? What are they?

D. Using the idioms from this unit or a previous one, develop a dialogue or role play about two people planning an activity. You may want to include the following:

- what activity they are planning;
- how they are planning it;
- whether anything has to remain undecided;
- whether anything is unacceptable to either person.

Unit 8
Chance and Opportunity

chances are (that) to be a good chance that something is true
also: **odds are (that)**

GRAMMAR NOTE: If *that* is not used, a comma follows each idiom.

- *Chances are that* the morning clouds will clear to sunny skies this afternoon.
- *Odds are*, you'll never see that unusual vocabulary word again.

be iffy to be questionable

GRAMMAR/USAGE NOTES: The verb *remain* can be used instead of *be*. The subject is sometimes a day of the week.

- It*'s iffy* whether we'll get a bonus this year, because company profits are down.
- The construction of the new highway through the middle of town *remains* very *iffy.*
- Friday *is iffy* for a game of baseball. Can we do it next Monday?

long shot an unlikely occurrence, something that has little chance of happening

- It's a *long shot* that Elaine will get admitted to Harvard with only a 3.4 grade average.
- Millions of people buy lottery tickets each year, but winning is a *long shot.*

stand a chance to be possible, to have the possibility of achieving
also: **have a ghost of a chance**

GRAMMAR/USAGE NOTES: Both expressions are usually followed by the preposition *of* and a gerund (verb + *-ing*). They may also be used in negative form when there is little possibility of something.

- The Altmont High School baseball team *stands a* good *chance* of winning the championship.
- Mr. Wilson does*n't have a ghost of a chance* of surviving another heart operation.

put all one's eggs in one basket to place all one's faith or money in one action or situation

- It's not wise to *put all your eggs in one basket* at an early age. Keep your career options open as long as possible.
- Mike *put all his eggs in one basket* when he bet a thousand dollars on one hand of blackjack.

irons in the fire   many activities or options at one time

USAGE NOTE: This expression applies to people who are actively pursuing many options in life.

- Gina is pursuing a musical career, a sports career, and a professional career all at the same time. She's got many *irons in the fire.*

pass up   to choose to miss an opportunity, to forego

GRAMMAR/USAGE NOTES: This idiom is separable and is often used with the noun *chance* or *opportunity.*

- How can you *pass up* the chance to meet your favorite author at the book signing?
- Ms. Forbes was offered a better job in another city, but she *passed* it *up* in order to stay near her family.

pipe dream   an impossible hope or expectation

- You can study acting as long as you like, but starring in a Hollywood movie is just a *pipe dream.*
- Greg should give up his *pipe dreams* and focus on the realities of life, such as getting a job.

miss the boat   to lose or miss a good opportunity

USAGE NOTE: This expression is used for opportunities that will probably not be available again.

- We really *missed the boat* when we didn't buy that real estate property. Now it's worth twice what we would have paid a year ago.
- Elyse *missed the boat* when she didn't accept the music scholarship.

miss out (on)   to lose an opportunity to do something

- Farah should have come with us to that fascinating presentation. She really *missed out.*
- That was a nice holiday party we had last week. I'm sorry that you *missed out on* it.

EXERCISES

A.   Fill in each blank with the appropriate form of an idiom from this unit. Some sentences may have more than one correct answer.

1. The weather forecaster says that the storm will probably bypass our area. In other words, the possibility of rain today is a _____ _____.

2. Jen still hopes that she can make the Olympic swim team at her age. Personally, I think it's better that she give up her _____ _____.

3. You're always busy with so many projects. How many _____ _____ _____ _____ do you have at the moment?

4. I wonder why Jorge didn't invest money in the valuable biotechnology stock recommended to him. He really _____ _____ _____.

5. When Bill was offered an excellent promotion that required moving overseas, he _____ _____ the opportunity because of his family.

6. Jake doesn't _____ _____ _____ of winning the spelling contest because he's not that good a speller.

7. There's a great sale at Martin's Department Store this Saturday. Let's get there early so we don't _____ _____ _____ the best specials.

(continued on next page)

8. Nicki said that she'll try to make it to the staff meeting today, but _____ _____ _____ she won't be able to.

9. It's advisable to apply to several graduate schools, not just one. Don't _____ _____ _____ _____ _____ _____ _____.

10. The defendant's attorney presented such a good case that it _____ very _____ whether the jury will convict.

B. Choose the statement in the right column that best responds to each question in the left column. Write the appropriate number in the blank.

1. Why did you pass up the chance to participate in the talent show?

2. Isn't it a long shot that Nancy can write a best-selling novel?

3. Does Mike stand a chance of being promoted to a supervisory position?

4. Are you going to miss out on our mountain hike this weekend?

5. Did Henry miss the boat by not investing in that stock fund?

____ a. Probably, but she's got other irons in the fire if she can't.

____ b. I don't think so. Chances are that others are more qualified.

____ c. Because it's just a pipe dream to think that I can act.

____ d. Yes, in hindsight he should have put all his eggs in one basket.

____ e. Saturday is iffy, but I could join you on Sunday.

C. Use the idioms in your spoken or written answers to the following questions.

1. Do you have many *irons in the fire* right now? What are they?

2. Have you ever *missed the boat* on doing something unusual or exciting? What was it?

3. Why might you *pass up* an opportunity to go rock climbing? To see an opera?

4. What kind of person *stands a chance* of becoming leader of a country? Do you *have a ghost of a chance* of accomplishing this? Why or why not?

5. What is the problem with *putting all your eggs in one basket?* Have you ever done this? What happened?

D. Using the idioms from this unit or a previous one, tell a classmate about something that you're trying to accomplish in your life. You may want to include the following:

- what you want to accomplish;
- what you think your chances of accomplishing it are;
- how you are approaching the situation;
- why you feel that you should make the effort no matter what happens.

Unit 9
Cooperation and Favor

pull together   to work together for a common purpose
- The city residents *pulled together* to rebuild the community after the devastating earthquake.
- If we *pull together,* we can accomplish the task in half the time.

put our/your/their heads together   to cooperate to find a solution

GRAMMAR NOTE: The possessive adjective is always plural.
- The doctors *put their heads together* to find a way to save the patient's life.
- We should be able to solve the mystery if we *put our heads together.*

take turns   to alternate in doing something
related form: **in turn** (adverb)

USAGE NOTE: *Take turns* is often followed by a gerund (verb + *-ing*) form.
- The children *took turns* playing with the new remote-controlled race car.
- The service desk personnel assisted customers waiting for refunds *in turn.*

play ball (with)   to cooperate
also: **work with**

USAGE NOTE: These idioms are used when someone is reluctant to help in the beginning.
- The crime witness wouldn't cooperate with the police at first, but after a talk with her lawyer, she agreed to *play ball.*
- It would be a lot easier if you *worked with me* rather than against me.

bend over backwards   to make extra effort to help or satisfy someone
also: **go out of one's way to**
- Carolyn has *bent over backwards* to satisfy her mother, and now it appears that she has agreed to do far too much.
- The contractor *went out of his way to* accommodate the wishes of the homeowner, but nothing seemed to be satisfactory.

It takes two to tango.   Cooperation is necessary to accomplish something.

USAGE NOTE: This expression is used when one or more persons are hesitant to cooperate.
- We'll never arrive at an agreement if you aren't willing to compromise. *It takes two to tango,* you know.

do a favor   to do something to help someone

> GRAMMAR NOTE: Either an object is placed after *do*, or a prepositional phrase starting with *for* is used.

- Could you *do* me *a favor?* I need another piece of tape, but my hands are full.
- Joey got five dollars because he *did a favor* for a neighbor.

real sport   someone who cooperates or does a favor willingly

- You're a *real sport* for helping me move all my belongings to the new apartment.
- I can't believe that Hank drove his roommate all the way to the airport. He's a *real sport.*

EXERCISES

A.   **Fill in each blank with the appropriate form of an idiom from this unit.**

JOSÉ: Hi, Gail. Could you _____ me _____ _____?

                                                1

GAIL: What is it, José?

JOSÉ: Could you possibly give me a ride to the airport tomorrow?

GAIL: Sure, I'd be glad to.

JOSÉ: You're a _____ _____, Gail. Say, can I help you address these

                          2

announcements about the ski trip?

GAIL: Oh, that's OK, José. You've _____ _____ _____ to help me so many

                                      3

times before.

JOSÉ: Well, I don't mind helping again. I have an idea. Let's _____ _____

                                            4

doing it.

GAIL: OK. I'll take a break and check where Nathan is.

JOSÉ: That's right—where is Nathan?

GAIL: He won't _____ _____ _____ me these days. I feel like I've been

                              5

working all alone.

JOSÉ: What's his problem?

GAIL: He thinks that I make too many decisions for the club on my own and ignore

others' opinions.

JOSÉ: That's ridiculous. We've always _____ _____ to accomplish tasks.

                                            6

Everyone knows that _____ _____ _____ _____ _____.

                                            7

GAIL: And that three or four are even better! Anyway, did you know that there's a

problem with the computer printer?

JOSÉ: Oh, what is it?

GAIL: I'm not sure, but it won't print out the labels properly. I was hoping that we

could _____ _____ _____ _____ to solve the problem.
₈

JOSÉ: Neither of us knows much about computers, but we can try!

B. Choose the statement in the right column that best responds to each question in the left column. Write the appropriate number in the blank.

1. Why should I go out of my way to help you this time?

_____ a. Yes, they quickly realized that it took two to tango.

2. Is John going to work with you on solving the financial matter?

_____ b. Not necessarily. In small groups they can put their heads together.

3. Shouldn't each student complete a project and present a report in turn?

_____ c. Because I did you a big favor just the other day!

_____ d. Yes, he's agreed to play ball in finding a solution.

4. Wasn't Paula a real sport to help us find a new apartment?

_____ e. Yes, she really bent over backwards to make time for us.

5. Did Carl and Joe finally pull together to complete the repairs in time?

C. Use the idioms in your spoken or written answers to the following questions.

1. When was the last time that you and a friend *pulled together* to solve a problem?
2. What kind of activity would you do *in turn* with others?
3. Has anyone been a *real sport* for you recently? What did he or she do?
4. What might you do for another person who *bent over backwards* to help you?
5. How do governments *work with* each other to solve the world's problems? Do you think they do enough? Why or why not?

D. Using the idioms from this unit or a previous one, develop a dialogue or role play about two or more friends trying to cooperate in solving a problem. You may want to include the following:

- why the friends need to cooperate;
- who cooperates willingly;
- whether anyone refuses to cooperate;
- how the problem is solved;
- whether any special effort is involved.

Unit 10
Luck, Hope, and Optimism

break a leg   to have good luck in the future

> GRAMMAR/USAGE NOTES: This idiom generally occurs in a command form and is used to wish someone good luck. The meaning of the expression is opposite the meaning of the individual words.
>
> ■ I just heard that your acting audition is today. I hope you get the part. **Break a leg!**
> ■ Kay told Manuel to **break a leg** in the 20K race.

luck out   to have unexpected luck or good fortune

> ■ Paul really **lucked out** on the test. He hardly studied and he still got an *A*.
> ■ The Mandelas **lucked out** when they got to the theater late and there were still good seats.

keep one's fingers crossed   to hope for good luck

> GRAMMAR/USAGE NOTES: This idiom usually occurs in a command form and is used when someone is concerned whether or not a situation actually happens.
>
> ■ **Keep your fingers crossed** that the travel agent can find you a flight at this late date.
> ■ It's rather cloudy for our picnic. We'll have to **keep our fingers crossed** that it doesn't rain.

wishful thinking   believing that something is true or possible when it really isn't

> ■ It's just **wishful thinking** for Hannah to believe that she can make the swim team. She isn't that good a swimmer.
> ■ Stop your **wishful thinking** and be glad for what you *do* have instead of always wanting more.

hope for the best   to be optimistic about the outcome of a situation

> ■ There's nothing we can do to change the mistake now. We can only **hope for the best.**
> ■ The parents of the sailors lost at sea had to **hope for the best** when the weather turned bad and the search was suspended.

hold out hope   to remain hopeful even when a situation looks bad

> USAGE NOTE: This idiom is usually used when there is a serious or life-threatening situation.
>
> ■ Everyone was **holding out hope** that more survivors of the terrible avalanche would be found.
> ■ The parents of the critically ill patient, **holding out hope** for a kidney transplant, have contacted all the donor banks across the country.

28

not be the end of the world   not be a reason to lose optimism
- Losing your job *is not the end of the world.* You've got enough qualifications and experience to find another one easily.

be looking up   to be improving or promising
USAGE NOTE: The plural form *things* is often used as the subject.
- Now that my health has returned to normal, my life *is looking up* again.
- After a brief downturn in the economy, things *are looking up* on the stock market.

The sky's the limit.   There is no limit to what someone can achieve.
GRAMMAR NOTE: The verb *be* is usually used in contracted form.
- For a person who has talent and works hard to achieve goals, *the sky's the limit.*
- When I asked about advancement within the new organization, the interviewer responded, *"The sky's the limit!"*

Every cloud has a silver lining.   Something good can come from something bad.
- Perhaps when you recover from your muscle injury, you'll be more dedicated to proper training. You see, *every cloud has a silver lining.*

EXERCISES

A.   **Fill in each blank with the appropriate form of an idiom from this unit.**

1. It's just _____ _____ to expect to win a major sweepstakes contest and become instantaneously rich.

2. As I was leaving the apartment to go to a job interview, my roommate shouted after me, "_____ _____ _____!"

3. The mountain rescue-team members _____ _____ _____ that they would find survivors when they reached the remote site of the plane crash.

4. Can you believe that Jennifer scored three goals to win the game for us? We really _____ _____ this time.

5. If you work hard and pursue your dream relentlessly, _____ _____ _____ _____.

6. It's too early to accurately forecast the weather for the day of the marathon race. The long-range forecast does give reason to _____ _____ _____ _____, though.

7. There are plenty of weeks left in the semester, so a *D* on one test is _____ _____ _____ _____ _____ _____.

8. The pain of my divorce is still with me, but I keep hoping that _____ _____ _____ _____ _____ _____.

9. The ex-convict feels that things _____ _____ _____ in his life now that he's found a job and lost his interest in easy money.

10. The engine of the car doesn't sound too good. We'll have to _____ _____ _____ _____ that it doesn't break down.

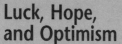

B. Choose the statement in the right column that best responds to each question in the left column. Write the appropriate number in the blank.

1. Isn't it great that things are looking up for you now?

2. Do you still hold out hope that we'll find our dog Ralph?

3. Is there any chance that we'll luck out and get tickets for good seats?

4. Isn't it terrible that I told Ted to break a leg, and then he actually did?

5. Is it wishful thinking to believe that five years in jail will help Kevin overcome his problems?

____ a. We can only keep looking for him and hope for the best.

____ b. Yes, I certainly feel that the sky's the limit!

____ c. Not if you believe that every cloud has a silver lining.

____ d. I'd keep my fingers crossed that the concert isn't sold out!

____ e. It's not the end of the world, though. He can still heal before basketball season.

C. Use the idioms in your spoken or written answers to the following questions.

1. Can you give some examples of situations in which you would *keep your fingers crossed?*

2. Can you describe a time when things were *looking up* in your life?

3. What are some ways that someone might *luck out* while traveling on vacation?

4. How would you help someone to see that a difficult situation *is not the end of the world?*

5. Is it just *wishful thinking* to believe that someday there will be world peace? Why or why not?

D. Using the idioms from this unit or a previous one, develop a dialogue or role play about two co-workers who have recently lost their jobs. You may want to include the following:

- why they lost their jobs;
- whether there's any hope of getting the jobs back;
- what attitude they have toward the present situation;
- how they feel about the future.

Review: Units 1-10

A. Circle the expression that best completes each sentence.

1. Why are you _____? We've got plenty of time to catch the train.
   - a. in a hurry
   - b. on the double
   - c. at a snail's pace

2. I thought you said that we should meet at John's house, not Alan's house. I guess we _____
   - a. got our wires crossed
   - b. jumped the gun
   - c. were up in the air

3. The publishing company is about to _____ a new book on exploring the World Wide Web.
   - a. mix up
   - b. go through
   - c. bring out

4. Even though I _____ to help Joe, he didn't even thank me afterwards.
   - a. bent over backwards
   - b. missed the boat
   - c. picked up

5. There was only one computer, so the students had to _____ using it.
   - a. pass up
   - b. take turns
   - c. slip up

6. The billionaire is glad to contribute a few thousand dollars to the charity because it's just _____ for him.
   - a. a drop in the bucket
   - b. the lion's share
   - c. irons in the fire

7. If you keep working hard and don't give up, you'll succeed _____.
   - a. to this day
   - b. all told
   - c. in the long run

8. I think that the worst of my problems are over, so things _____ in my life.
   - a. are iffy
   - b. are on the wrong track
   - c. are looking up

9. The young pianist was _____ just before she went on stage to perform.
   - a. wishful thinking
   - b. on pins and needles
   - c. playing it by ear

10. Isn't Elaine's hope to become a famous movie star just _____?
    - a. a real sport
    - b. a pipe dream
    - c. a slip of the tongue

B. Indicate whether each statement is TRUE (T) or FALSE (F).

_____ 1. If you have only a few dollars, you might come up short when paying for something.

_____ 2. To not miss a beat is to get mixed up.

_____ 3. When you're not thinking straight, you might goof up.

_____ 4. If you tell someone to shake a leg, then you're suggesting they slow down.

_____ 5. Two people might put their heads together to map out a plan.

_____ 6. If you've been dragging your heels to accomplish something, then you might have to do it at the last minute.

_____ 7. Chances are that you can learn all of the idioms in this book in no time.

_____ 8. A pack rat probably has many things that are collecting dust.

_____ 9. You might rule out something that's a long shot.

_____ 10. If you tell someone to break a leg, then you're hoping for the best.

C. Complete the puzzle with the missing parts of the idioms in the sentences below.

ACROSS

2. How did Tom _____ up a scheme like that?
3. Could you do me a _____ and answer the doorbell?
5. Don't put all your eggs in one _____ .
11. All of a _____ it began to rain hard.
12. The traffic is heavy, so please _____ down.
13. On the spur of the _____ we went out to eat.
15. That constant noise is starting to try my _____ .
16. Hold your _____ ! There's no hurry to leave.

DOWN

1. Ann doesn't stand a _____ of getting that job.
2. Every _____ has a silver lining.
4. Go to your room and study right _____ !
6. By pulling _____ , we can get it done faster.
7. Let's keep our _____ crossed that it works.
8. There are at _____ a hundred people in here.
9. We need to buy a _____ of items at the store.
10. I really stuck my foot in my _____ .
14. It takes two to _____ , you know.

32

Unit 11
Human Relations

make friends   to become good friends with others

> USAGE NOTE: This idiom is used to describe people who are either quite sociable or not very sociable at all.

- Edward *makes friends* very easily. That's why he's the most popular person in the office.
- Why is it so hard for me to *make friends?* Do you think that I have an unfriendly personality?

hit it off   to develop a friendly relationship quickly

> GRAMMAR NOTE: The pronoun *it* cannot be substituted or changed in any way.

- Isabel knew that she would marry Umberto some day because they *hit it off* right from the start.
- Brett and Linda's first date was a disaster. They didn't *hit it off* at all.

start off on the wrong foot   to have a bad start to a relationship
opposite meaning: **start off on the right foot**   to have a good start

> USAGE NOTE: The verb *get* can also be used.

- I know we *started off on the wrong foot* because I was late on our first date, but could you please give me another chance?
- The first day on the job, Ray *got off on the right foot* by impressing his boss with some good decision making.

get along (with)   to interact well or associate (with)

> USAGE NOTE: This idiom is used to indicate whether or not there is a friendly relationship.

- Patricia quit the track team because she and her coach didn't *get along* at all.
- The Jensens' children don't *get along with* each other very well, so they each have their own bedroom.

rub elbows (with)   to interact socially (with)

> USAGE NOTE: This idiom is used when someone interacts with important or interesting people.

- The business convention was a good chance for the entrepreneur to gain knowledge and *rub elbows.*
- The aspiring actor was delighted to be invited to a party where he could *rub elbows with* some important directors and producers.

face to face   directly, in each other's presence

> GRAMMAR NOTE: Hyphens (-) are used when the idiom is an adjective preceding a noun.

- After knowing you only by phone for the last week, it's nice to finally meet you *face to face.*
- James and his mother had a *face-to-face* talk about his disrespectful attitude toward adults.

tie the knot   to get married

> also: **get hitched**

> USAGE NOTE: These idioms are used informally and often when the decision to marry is a quick one.

- Some couples fly off to Las Vegas to *tie the knot.* Many of those marriages don't last very long.
- After years of dating, Marj and Henry have decided to *get hitched.*

on the rocks   troubled (when having to do with relationships)

- The Sadoudis are seeing a counselor because their marriage is *on the rocks.*
- It's possible to save a relationship that's *on the rocks* through understanding and compromise.

EXERCISES

A.   **Fill in each blank with the appropriate form of an idiom from this unit.**

1. It's not appropriate to discuss this matter over the phone. Let's meet tomorrow and discuss it _____ _____ _____.

2. Melinda and her boyfriend _____ _____ _____ at a small wedding chapel near Niagara Falls.

3. My new roommate and I are the best of friends. We really _____ _____ _____ from the start.

4. Do you _____ _____ _____ your younger brother, or do you constantly argue and fight like many brothers?

5. Frank and Gina were invited to the Beverly Hills party where they were able to _____ _____ _____ some well-known Hollywood personalities.

6. When Larry moved to another city, he joined a health club so that he could exercise and _____ _____ at the same time.

7. Isn't it a shame that the Underhill's marriage is _____ _____ _____? They'll probably divorce very soon.

8. Even though we _____ _____ _____ _____ _____ _____, let's try to be friendly from now on.

B. Choose the statement in the right column that best responds to each question in the left column. Write the appropriate number in the blank.

1. Did you and Carol start off on the right foot on your first date?

2. Were you able to rub elbows with some politicians at the election party?

3. Do you know why the Burtons' marriage is already on the rocks?

4. Why have Matt and Bianca decided to tie the knot so soon?

5. Why is it so difficult for Miguel to make friends with others?

____ a. They hit it off perfectly from the start.

____ b. Yes, and I even met the city mayor face to face.

____ c. No, I'm sorry to say that she and I got off on the wrong foot.

____ d. I'm not sure, but he's always had trouble getting along with others.

____ e. I think it's because they got hitched at an early age.

C. Use the idioms in your spoken or written answers to the following questions.

1. For what reasons might you *hit it off* with someone? Has this ever happened to you? Explain.

2. For what reasons might you *start off on the wrong foot* with someone? Has this ever happened to you? Explain.

3. Do you *get along with* your brothers and sisters? Your parents? Is there anyone that you don't *get along with*?

4. Have you already *tied the knot*? If not, do you plan to *get hitched* some day? Why or why not?

5. Have you ever *rubbed elbows* with a famous or influential person? If so, who was it? If not, would you like to? Who with?

D. Using the idioms from this unit or a previous one, develop a dialogue or role play about a counselor advising a couple who are having marital problems. You may want to include the following:

- when the couple got married;
- how the relationship was in the beginning;
- the cause of the present marital difficulty;
- how the couple associate with each other;
- how the couple deal with their problems.

Unit 12
Character Traits

thick-skinned   not easily angered or bothered by something
opposite meaning: **thin-skinned**

- A sports referee has to be *thick-skinned* in order to ignore the comments of players and fans.
- Nathan reacts to every little criticism about him. He's too *thin-skinned* for his own good.

soft-hearted   unable to refuse the requests of others
related form: **a soft touch** (noun phrase)

- Deirdre gives some money to every homeless person she sees. She's too *soft-hearted.*
- The children know that their grandmother is *a soft touch,* so they're always asking for special treats.

hot-headed   easily angered

- The fight happened because the girls became *hot-headed* over nothing.
- Why do you get so *hot-headed* when your assistant makes a mistake? He's doing his best, you know.

be out of character   not be typical of someone's usual character
opposite meaning: **be in character**
USAGE NOTE: This idiom is usually followed by a *for/to* infinitive phrase.

- It*'s out of character* for Jake to dance wildly like that. He's usually so conservative.
- Unfortunately, Julie *is in character* when she talks only about herself. It's unusual for her to be interested in the affairs of others.

live wire   a very energetic person
USAGE NOTE: The words *such a* often precede this idiom.

- You must have gotten a lot of sleep last night. You're such a *live wire* today.
- Age has slowed down Mr. Evans, who has always been known as something of a *live wire.*

tough cookie   someone who has a strong or stubborn character
USAGE NOTE: The word *one* or *a* often precedes this idiom.

- Of anyone I know, Omar can handle a challenging situation the best. He's one *tough cookie.*
- We all tried to change Irma's mind, but she wouldn't listen. She's a *tough cookie.*

36

stick in the mud   a boring, uninteresting person
    also: **bump on a log**
    USAGE NOTE: These idioms are often preceded by *such a.*
    ▪ How can you refuse to go to the show with all your friends? Don't be such a *stick in the mud.*
    ▪ Mr. Kaplan is becoming such a *bump on a log.* His wife goes out, and he just stays home and tinkers in his garage.

have a (good) head on one's shoulders   to be an intelligent thinker
    ▪ Everyone knows that Marcia will succeed in life because she *has a head on her shoulders.*
    ▪ Mom and Dad, you're the reason that I *have a good head on my shoulders.*

soft in the head   not intelligent, dumb
    ▪ I don't know why Ralph keeps calling me "Doug" when my name is "Don." He must be *soft in the head.*
    ▪ Isn't Jules a little *soft in the head?* No one would make the same mistake three times!

EXERCISES

A.   Fill in each blank with the appropriate form of an idiom from this unit. Some sentences may have more than one correct answer.

1. Karen was accepted to the Massachusetts Institute of Technology because she

    _____ _____ _____ _____ _____ _____ _____.

2. Paul always talks and acts fast. If anyone can be called a _____ _____, it's him.

3. I made only one comment to Debbie, and then she got all _____ - _____ and started shouting at me.

4. How could you possibly agree to buy the children another video game so soon? You're just too _____ - _____.

5. Ursula is usually such a composed person, so it _____ _____ _____ _____ for her to have cried at the wedding.

6. Nothing anyone says ever seems to bother you. You're so _____ - _____.

7. Why would Hans try to ride his bike to school through heavy snow? He must be a little _____ _____ _____ _____.

8. Wanda kept playing soccer even though her ankle was sprained and her thigh was bruised. She's one _____ _____.

9. Everyone wants to go to the beach except for you. How can you be such a

    _____ _____ _____ _____?

B. Choose the statement in the right column that best responds to each question in the left column. Write the appropriate number in the blank.

1. Is it in character for Ann to dance wildly like that?

2. Why does Lynne often get hot-headed for little reason?

3. Have you ever known a person as thick-skinned as Mr. Hansen?

4. Why is Dave such a bump on a log about doing anything new and exciting?

5. Isn't Mrs. Wilson being unusually soft-hearted to let the kids play in her big tree?

____ a. No, I've never met such a tough cookie before, either.

____ b. No, she's usually not such a live wire.

____ c. I think it's because he's a little soft in the head.

____ d. She's one of the most thin-skinned persons I know.

____ e. It's out of character for her to let them into her yard at all.

C. Use the idioms in your spoken or written answers to the following questions.

1. *Is* it *in character* for you to be *thick-skinned* or *thin-skinned?* Explain.

2. What kinds of childhood experiences could turn a person into a *tough cookie?* Into a *soft touch?* What is true for you?

3. What would a *live wire* have difficulty doing? Do you ever have this same problem?

4. What kinds of things would a *stick in the mud* like to do? Do you ever feel this way?

5. How would you know that someone *had a good head on his or her shoulders?* Is it possible for everyone to be this way? Why or why not?

D. Using the idioms from this unit or a previous one, develop a presentation about your own character. You may want to include the following:

- your assessment of your intelligence;
- your tendencies toward expressing anger;
- how much energy you have;
- examples of behavior that reflect (or do not reflect) your true character.

Unit 13
Modern Life

dog-eat-dog world   a very competitive and often unfair world

USAGE NOTE: This idiom can be used when people resort to almost any means to achieve their goals.

- Did you hear that over 300 people applied for the entry-level job at Monty's Department Store? It's a ***dog-eat-dog world*** out there!
- It says in the newspaper that 500 senior citizens were cheated out of over $3 million by a telemarketing firm. What a ***dog-eat-dog world!***

rat race   the continual struggle to survive in life

- Charlene has had enough of the ***rat race.*** She's quitting her job and buying a ranch in Montana.
- Some people move to the country in order to avoid the ***rat race*** of city life.

on the run   always moving, never resting
also: **on the go**

- Sorry I don't have time to talk with you very often. It seems that I'm always ***on the run.***
- Lisa enjoys being ***on the go*** all the time. She likes to keep herself busy.

run around in circles   to be so busy that one isn't sure what to do next

- Look at me. I'm trying to do three things at once and I'm only managing to ***run around in circles!***
- The whole family was ***running around in circles*** getting the Thanksgiving dinner ready.

in a rut   in a boring or unchanging situation in life

USAGE NOTE: The word *such* can be added before *a*.

- You need to get out and make some new friends. There's no sense staying ***in a rut.***
- Tami and Alan seem to be ***in*** such ***a rut*** these days. They never have any interesting news to relate when I call them.

back to the same old grind   back to someone's usual work routine
also: **back to the grindstone**

USAGE NOTE: These idioms are usually used after a period of rest or vacation.

- That vacation was wonderful, but now it's ***back to the same old grind.***
- The workers took a ten-minute break and then went ***back to the grindstone.***

couch potato   someone who does a lot of sitting and watching TV

- On Sundays, millions of people become **couch potatoes** and watch professional sports events on TV.
- Every night Max comes home from work and turns into a **couch potato**. He doesn't even answer his phone!

creature comforts (of home)   the conveniences of modern life

- How did people survive fifty years ago when **creature comforts** such as air-conditioning were unavailable?
- Harriet moved into a modern apartment so that she could enjoy all the **creature comforts of home.**

keep up with the Joneses   to maintain the same lifestyle as one's friends and neighbors

USAGE NOTES: This idiom is used when someone is very aware of social status and possessions. Only the name *Jones* can be used.

- The Youngs just bought a new minivan even though they can't afford it. They have to **keep up with the Joneses,** you know.

EXERCISES

A.   Fill in each blank with the appropriate form of an idiom from this unit. Some sentences may have more than one correct answer.

PIA: Why are you leaving the office in such a hurry, Val?

VAL: It's the end of the workday, and I can't wait to get back to my apartment and enjoy the _____ _____ _____ _____!
                                    1

PIA: I understand. Were you very busy today?

VAL: Busy? I was _____ _____ _____ all day. Sometimes it seemed like I
                                    2

was _____ _____ _____ _____ and getting nothing done.
            3

PIA: You know, I hate this _____ _____ we face each day.
                                    4

VAL: I agree. It's a _____ - _____ - _____ _____ out there.
                            5

PIA: That's the truth. Besides, we're always struggling to _____ _____
                                                                6

_____ _____ _____—as if it really mattered.

VAL: I know what you mean. My problem is that I seem to be _____ _____
                                                                7

_____ at home.

PIA: Oh, how so?

VAL: Well, I've become somewhat of a _____ _____ sitting in front of the TV.
                                        8

PIA: That's too bad. You should really get out and do things on the weekends.

VAL: I know, but I don't. And then, before I know it, it's _____ _____
                                                            9

_____ _____ _____ _____ on Monday!

B.   Choose the statement in the right column that best responds to each question in the left column. Write the appropriate number in the blank.

1. Don't you often get tired of this dog-eat-dog world?

2. Why does it seem that you're always running around in circles?

3. Isn't it incredible how Nicholas has become such a couch potato?

4. Can't we take a break after being on the go for several hours?

5. Don't you think that our house is already equipped with enough creature comforts?

____ a. Yes. It's too bad that he's in such a rut these days.

____ b. I do, and the urge to escape the rat race grows greater each year.

____ c. Not if we want to keep up with the Joneses!

____ d. I guess it's because I'm constantly on the run.

____ e. OK, but after a ten-minute rest, it's back to the grindstone.

C.   Use the idioms in your spoken or written answers to the following questions.

1. Do you think it's a *dog-eat-dog world* out there? Why or why not?

2. What do you do to escape the *rat race* of everyday living?

3. Are you ever a *couch potato?* If so, do you enjoy being that way? Why or why not?

4. What *creature comforts* do you have in your home? Which ones do you still want to get?

5. Do you believe that it's important to *keep up with the Joneses?* Why or why not?

D.   Using the idioms from this unit or a previous one, develop a presentation about how you handle modern living. You may want to include the following:

- your normal work or study routine;
- how busy you are;
- how you use your free time;
- what you value most (or least) in life;
- your opinion of today's world.

Unit 14
Driving and Traffic

pull over   to drive to the side of the road; to cause to drive to the side of the road
related idiom: **pull off** to move off the road entirely; to cause to move off the road
GRAMMAR/USAGE NOTES: Both idioms can be used with or without an object. When an object is used, the idioms must be separated and are causative in nature. *Pull off* can be followed by another noun such as *road* or *highway*.

■ I hear a noise from the engine area. ***Pull over*** so I can check it.

■ We had to ***pull*** the car ***off*** the road to change a flat tire.

as far as   until reaching a certain place
USAGE NOTE: This idiom is usually followed by a noun phrase, or sometimes by a sentence.

■ Drive down this road ***as far as*** the first traffic light, and then turn left.

■ To get to the coliseum, you just continue down this highway ***as far as*** you can go.

pull in(to)   to leave the road and drive into a place to park
also: **turn in(to)**
USAGE NOTE: These idioms are followed by nouns such as *driveway, parking lot, garage,* and so on.

■ There's no reason to leave the car in the driveway overnight. It's better to ***pull into*** the garage.

■ There's the building. ***Turn in*** here and park anywhere you find a spot.

turn around   to reverse the direction of movement
GRAMMAR NOTE: This idiom can be used with or without an object and is separable.

■ Hank drove past the highway on-ramp and had to ***turn around*** and go back.

■ The delivery person ***turned*** the truck ***around*** and headed back up the road.

U-turn   reversal of direction
USAGE NOTE: This idiom often follows the verb *make*.

■ In some states it's legal to make a ***U-turn*** across broken double lines in the center of a street.

■ The officer ticketed the motorist for an illegal ***U-turn*** at the intersection.

fender bender   a small accident
- Police don't usually fill out accident reports on small *fender benders.* The motorists are expected to exchange essential information and contact their insurance companies.
- There are a lot of *fender benders* on southern California highways after the first rainstorm of the season, when drivers are not used to wet conditions.

bumper-to-bumper   very crowded and hardly moving on the highway
related idioms: **stack up, back up** (verbs)
GRAMMAR NOTE: *Stack up* and *back up* are usually used in passive form for this meaning.
- Oliver bought some new CDs to make the *bumper-to-bumper* commute to work more enjoyable.
- There's a serious accident blocking three lanes on route 880. Traffic is *stacked up* all the way back to the 90/505 interchange and should remain *backed up* for several hours.

stop and go   barely moving, congested
GRAMMAR NOTE: Hyphens (-) are used when the idiom precedes a noun.
- It took us twice as long to get to our destination because it was *stop and go* all the way.
- Automobiles wear out more quickly when they are exposed to *stop-and-go* traffic in the city.

up to speed   back to normal speed
USAGE NOTE: The word *back* often precedes this idiom.
- Traffic is *up to speed* now that the debris has been cleared from the highway.
- All vehicles slowed at the immigration checkpoint but were back *up to speed* after passing it.

wrap up   to end, to finish
GRAMMAR/USAGE NOTES: This idiom may be used with or without an object and is separable. It is used in this case to refer to an accident that is nearly removed from the highway. It can also be used for other kinds of events and activities.
- Police are just *wrapping up* at the accident scene and should be done in a few minutes.
- How soon will the emergency crews *wrap up* at the mess on the 503 freeway?
- OK, class, that *wraps* it *up.* You're free to leave early today.

EXERCISES

A.   **Fill in each blank with the appropriate form of an idiom from this unit. Some sentences may have more than one correct answer.**

1. Because the traffic signals on the main highway were not working properly, even the light traffic on the weekend was _____ _____ _____.

2. Sam is lucky that he can walk to work. He never has to commute in _____ - _____ - _____ traffic.

3. You deserve a traffic ticket for making an illegal _____ - _____ across the center median.

4. Keep going on this road _____ _____ _____ the next traffic light and then turn left.

(continued on next page)

5. I think we're driving in the wrong direction. Let's _____ _____ and go back.

6. Barbara couldn't believe that the small dent in her car from the _____ _____ could cost so much money to repair.

7. Taxi driver, this is where I need to get out. Please _____ _____ to the curb.

8. All lanes of traffic will be open again as soon as police and fire crews have _____ _____ the serious accident.

9. Could you _____ _____ this parking lot so that I can use the pay phone?

10. Only once in two hours did the traffic slow to a crawl, but after a short while we were back _____ _____ _____.

B. Choose the statement in the right column that best responds to each question in the left column. Write the appropriate number in the blank.

1. Why is the traffic suddenly backed up like this?

2. Are you going to try to make a U-turn in the middle of this busy street?

3. Should I pull into the driveway and park in the garage?

4. Don't you feel terrible about the small fender bender you just caused?

5. Why did we suddenly get back up to speed again without even passing an emergency?

____ a. Yes, but I can partially blame it on the stop-and-go traffic.

____ b. An accident must have wrapped up a little while ago.

____ c. How else do you expect me to turn the car around?

____ d. No, just pull over to the curb. I'm using the car later.

____ e. I don't know, but we'll have to stay on the highway as far as the next exit.

C. Use the idioms in your spoken or written answers to the following questions.

1. For what reasons would you *pull into* a gas station?

2. Why is it dangerous for you to make a *U-turn* in the middle of a crowded road?

3. If you had to commute to and from work every day, how could you learn whether the traffic was *bumper-to-bumper* or *up to speed?*

4. Have you ever been involved in a *fender bender?* What are you supposed to do in such a case?

5. Have you ever been *pulled over* by a police officer? For what offense?

D. Using the idioms from this unit or a previous one, develop a presentation about driving conditions in a city you know well. You may want to include the following:

- how the traffic generally is at different times of day;
- what kinds of accidents there are;
- how quickly emergency crews respond to an accident;
- the law regarding turns in the middle of the street.

Unit 15
Banking and Finance

make out (a check)   to write or fill in a check

> GRAMMAR NOTE: This idiom is separable, and the article *the* can be used.

- The company's name is Olsen Electric, but I'd prefer it if you *made out the check* to me.
- The total is five hundred dollars and sixty cents, but you can *make* it *out* for five hundred.

bounce a check   to pay by check without having enough money available in the checking account

- Kenneth doesn't have much money in his checking account, so he has to be careful not to *bounce a check.*
- Miriam *bounced a check* at the grocery store because she hadn't balanced her checkbook properly.

on credit   without having to pay with cash or with a check at the moment of purchase

- Many consumers buy *on credit* because it's easier to reach for a plastic charge card than to carry a lot of cash.
- We'll have to make a refund to your account because you paid for this *on credit.*

take out   to withdraw money from one's account; to arrange a loan from a financial institution

> GRAMMAR NOTE: This idiom is separable.

- An automatic teller machine, or ATM, makes it very easy to *take out* cash any time of the day or night.
- The Jacksons *took* a loan *out* to cover the cost of a down payment on a house.

pay off   to finish making payments on

> GRAMMAR/USAGE NOTES: This idiom is separable and often used in passive form. It is used for a credit card balance or personal loan.

- I can't wait until my credit card balance is all *paid off* in a couple of months. Then I can start saving for a vacation!
- When Mr. Evanston retired, he and his wife decided to *pay* the mortgage *off* so that they would own their home outright.

put aside   to save for a special purpose, to keep in reserve
also: **lay aside, set aside**

GRAMMAR NOTE: These idioms are separable.

- May's family *puts aside* a little bit every month toward her college tuition fund. Even May tries to *lay aside* some of her own money.
- Jamie has decided to **set** ten dollars *aside* each week toward the household expenses.

two bits   twenty-five cents
related expressions: **buck** (one dollar); **grand** (one thousand dollars)

GRAMMAR/USAGE NOTES: *Buck* and *grand* are single vocabulary words, but their meanings are idiomatic.

- I don't have any change. Do you have *two bits* for the parking meter?
- It would be nice to win a *grand* in the state lottery, but a hundred *bucks* would be better than nothing.

chip in   to contribute money

GRAMMAR NOTES: This idiom may be used with or without an object. It is generally not separated.

- When the Armstrongs' home was destroyed by fire, their neighbors *chipped in* to help with repairs.
- Everyone *chipped in* a few dollars to buy Anna some roses while she was recovering from the operation.

pay back   to return what is owed

GRAMMAR NOTE: This idiom is separable.

- Daniel never expects his friends to *pay back* the money that he lends them, because he's too wealthy to care.
- I still don't have the sixty dollars I owe you. Can I *pay* you *back* next week?

EXERCISES

A.   Fill in each blank with the appropriate form of an idiom from this unit. Some sentences may have more than one correct answer.

JAY: Ian, the bank just called to say that you _____ _____ _____ last
        1
week.

IAN: What? That's not possible. I only _____ _____ one check last week,
        2
and that was for twenty dollars.

JAY: You'll have to resolve the problem tomorrow. Instead of writing checks for your
purchases, you should buy _____ _____.
        3

IAN: No way. I'd charge too much and then have to _____ _____ another
        4
loan to cover the payments on my credit card balance.

JAY: There's nothing wrong with that. People do it all the time.

IAN: But I'm not going to. I just _____ _____ my car loan, and now I plan
        5
to _____ _____ a little money each month for a vacation.
    6

Jay: That sounds like a plan. Say, could you give me a couple of bucks so that I have

enough to buy a CD? I'll _____ _____ the money next week.
                        7

Ian: I don't care about that, but all I have is this one coin in my pocket—_____
                                                                              8

_____. Sorry I can't _____ _____ more!
                        9

B. Choose the statement in the right column that best responds to each question in the left column. Write the appropriate number in the blank.

1. How large was the loan that Julie took out from the bank?

2. Would you mind if I made out a check for my share of the carry-out food?

3. How much have you been able to lay aside for your daughter's education?

4. When is Peter going to pay back the money that he owes you?

5. Why are you making this purchase on credit?

____ a. The savings account has reached almost ten grand now.

____ b. Because I don't want to bounce another check!

____ c. Two thousand dollars. She'll be able to pay it off in five years.

____ d. Well, it would be easier if you chipped in cash.

____ e. I don't know, but it'll probably be a few bucks at a time.

C. Use the idioms in your spoken or written answers to the following questions.

1. For what purchases or activities might you agree to *chip in* some money with friends?

2. Do you ever buy things *on credit?* Is it easy or difficult for you to control the number of purchases you make this way? Why?

3. Have you ever *taken out* a loan? For what purpose? What future purchase might require you to do so?

4. What might happen if you were unable to *pay back* a loan to a financial institution?

5. Have you already *put aside* some money for future emergencies? Why or why not?

D. Using the idioms from this unit or a previous one, develop a dialogue or role play involving two persons discussing personal finances. You may want to include the following:

- each person's spending habits;
- each person's saving habits;
- recent financial arrangements;
- any financial problems.

Unit 16
Business and Employment

set up shop   to start a business
related idiom: **mom-and-pop operation** (a small family business)

- The florist moved into a new neighborhood and *set up shop* on a good street corner.
- *Mom-and-pop operations* are being threatened by superstores, which offer everything under one roof.

do business (with)   to have business transactions (with)

- Don't *do business with* that repair shop. I'm sure they cheated me the last time.
- Thanks for buying your new insurance policy through our company. It's been nice *doing business with* you.

head-hunter   someone who recruits highly qualified candidates for a job

DEFINITION NOTE: A *head-hunter* is a special person that a company hires to find suitable candidates for a position.

- The government physicist wasn't thinking of changing jobs to the private sector, but a *head-hunter* convinced her it would be financially worthwhile.

household word   a well-known brand, a well-known company name
also: **household name**

- Every company hopes that the new products that they introduce each year will become *household words.*
- Smith Consolidated is a *household name* for many Americans because the company has over six hundred stores in the East and Midwest.

on the market   available to the public in stores

- The most difficult part for the inventors was getting their new game *on the market.*
- With the enormous selection of food products *on the market,* there's intense competition for shelf space in stores.

go out of business   to fail as a business, to stop operations
also: **go under**

- Two small video stores *went out of business* in our neighborhood when a large video chain opened a store nearby.
- Do you know that over 75 percent of all new businesses *go under* within the first year of operation?

48

rank and file   common workers in a factory or business

> GRAMMAR NOTE: Hyphens (-) are added when this idiom is used as an adjective.

- One purpose of a union is to represent the ***rank and file*** in salary negotiations.
- The ***rank-and-file*** workers were opposed to the cut in benefits proposed by management.

put in for   to apply for, to request

> USAGE NOTE: This idiom is usually followed by a noun such as *job, position,* or *transfer.*

- A dozen people ***put in for*** the dean's position when she announced her retirement last month.
- As soon as the Tokyo branch opens, Val intends to ***put in for*** a transfer there.

lay off   to release from a job, to discharge
also: **give the pink slip**

> GRAMMAR NOTE: Both idioms are separable and often used in passive form.

- In order to increase profits and the value of stock, the company ***laid off*** over 200 workers whose positions had become automated.
- Without warning, Mr. Quincy was ***given the pink slip*** after over thirty years of service.

go on strike   to refuse to work for some special reason
also: **walk off the job**

- The construction workers ***went on strike*** when another serious accident happened at the unsafe job site.
- As soon as the union deadline passed at midnight, all transportation workers ***walked off the job.***

EXERCISES

A.   Fill in each blank with the appropriate form of an idiom from this unit. Some sentences may have more than one correct answer.

The name Baldwin's Pride has been a _____ _____ across the
                                                          1
United States for more than a century, ever since Elijah Baldwin _____
                                                                          2
_____ _____ in a small Boston warehouse in 1878. The company, known
as Baldwin Manufacturing, has had many best-selling products _____
                                                                          3
_____ _____. Over the years the company has developed a fine reputation
for _____ _____ the old-fashioned way.
      4
Recently, however, the company had to _____ _____ hundreds of
                                                      5
_____ - _____ - _____ workers in an effort to lower costs. Without
      6
major reductions in salaries, the company faced the real possibility of _____
                                                                                7
_____ _____ _____.

However, the workers didn't accept the company's actions, so they
_____ _____ _____. After weeks of demonstrations and picketing, the
      8

(continued on next page)

company director resigned, and a _____ - _____ was hired to find a
                                          9
replacement director. It was indeed fortunate that a well-qualified person

_____ _____ _____ the position and was hired right away. As a result,
        10

progress is now being made on a settlement to the strike.

B. Choose the statement in the right column that best responds to each question in the left column. Write the appropriate number in the blank.

1. How do you like the new owners of the mom-and-pop business on the corner?
2. Why did the company give the pink slip to so many employees?
3. What did the rank and file decide in the union strike vote?
4. Did they have to hire a head-hunter to find a qualified operations officer?
5. How many products does that new retail company have on the market now?

____ a. Enough to have become a household word.
____ b. They want to walk off the job at the end of the week.
____ c. It was either take that action or eventually go under.
____ d. So far it's been a pleasure doing business with them.
____ e. No, someone from within the company put in for the position.

C. Use the idioms in your spoken or written answers to the following questions.

1. What are some *household words* either in the United States or in a country you know well?
2. Some people think that there are too many products of the same kind *on the market.* Do you agree? Why or why not?
3. Why might a company be forced to *go out of business?*
4. What happens to someone who is *laid off?* Has this ever happened to you or to someone you know?
5. For what reasons might factory workers want to *go on strike?*

D. Using the idioms from this unit or a previous one, develop a presentation about a real or imagined retail business that's having financial difficulties or labor troubles. You may want to include the following:

- what kind of business it is;
- how many workers it has;
- how the business sells its products;
- the nature of its financial difficulties or labor troubles;
- if the jobs of any workers are at risk.

Unit 17
Government and Politics

run for (the) office (of)   to enter a political race (for)
related idiom: **toss one's hat into the ring** (to announce that one is entering a political campaign)

- The governor of New York announced that he is *running for the office of* president of the United States.
- With her questionable background and poor track record, the city manager shouldn't *run for office* again.
- The local political activist considered tossing *her hat into the ring* for the county board of supervisors after the board made a series of questionable decisions.

press the flesh   to shake hands with the public while campaigning for office

- Some politicians love *pressing the flesh* in political campaigns, while others detest the process of meeting so many voters.
- The leading candidate for mayor *pressed the flesh* with hundreds of supporters at the fund-raising picnic.

sound bite   a statement made by a politician that is widely quoted by the media
USAGE NOTE: This idiom is used when a politician makes a brief statement that the media finds interesting and uses.

- The following *sound bite* was taken from a Texas congressman's response to a question about the possibility of a tax increase: "There will be no new taxes in Texas!"
- The statement "Over my dead body!" makes for an interesting *sound bite,* but is it a realistic attitude to take?

take office   to officially begin a term as a politician
related idiom: **swear in** (to administer an oath to someone beginning a political term)
GRAMMAR NOTE: *Swear in* is separable.

- The president-elect gave a wonderful inaugural speech on the day he *took office.*
- A justice of the Supreme Court usually *swears* the president *in* on Inauguration Day.

middle-of-the-road   moderate in one's political beliefs
related idioms: **left-wing** (liberal); **right-wing** (conservative)
GRAMMAR NOTE: These idioms are used as adjective forms.

- Ms. Grey has been elected to the school board because she takes a *middle-of-the-road* approach to solving problems.
- Most *right-wing* citizens in the United States vote Republican, while most *left-wing* citizens vote Democrat.

51

party line   the principles of a political party that all members are expected to follow

- The reporter talked to several different Republican members of Congress, but all she got was the *party line.*
- Several legislators departed from the *party line* and voted to increase educational spending.

red tape   bureaucratic paperwork caused by overregulation

USAGE NOTE: This idiom often follows the verbal idiom *go through.*

- The county government had to go through a lot of *red tape* in order to obtain emergency funds from the federal government.
- There's a lot of *red tape* involved in obtaining a government loan for a new small business.

grass-roots   of or by common people

GRAMMAR/USAGE NOTES: This idiom is used as an adjective phrase and refers to the efforts of citizens to affect the political process directly.

- Many environmental concerns are championed by *grass-roots* organizations such as the Sierra Club.
- The corrupt politician was removed from office because of a *grass-roots* recall campaign.

EXERCISES

A.   **Fill in each blank with the appropriate form of an idiom from this unit.**

1. While most of my friends are either left-wing or right-wing, I take a more _____ - _____ - _____ - _____ stance.

2. Janet Thompson will step down as mayor on January 3 and the mayor-elect will _____ _____ the same day.

3. "Stop government interference in our lives" is a wonderful _____ _____ on the TV news, but in reality it's an impractical position to take.

4. Why did Republican representative Tom Kresge depart from the _____ _____ and vote with the Democrats on that bill?

5. Small businesses spend a lot of time dealing with all the _____ _____ created by local, state, and federal governments.

6. The Madisons were so disenchanted with the local school system that they joined a _____ - _____ organization to reform it.

7. The incumbent politician was unopposed in the election because no one else would _____ _____ _____ against her.

8. Lars Freeman is a consummate politician. He loves to walk among people in the crowds and _____ _____ _____.

B. Choose the statement in the right column that best responds to each question in the left column. Write the appropriate number in the blank.

1. How's that grass-roots organization you joined?

2. Has Mary Allison been sworn in as governor yet?

3. Was there anything interesting to learn from yesterday's sound bites?

4. Is our local representative running for the office of state senator?

5. Who's to blame for all the red tape in government these days?

____ a. No, she doesn't take office until tomorrow.

____ b. Hardly. Everyone was just repeating the party line.

____ c. Unfortunately, the group is too middle-of-the-road for me.

____ d. Right-wing politicians like to blame left-wingers for it.

____ e. Yes, she tossed her hat into the ring at a news conference this morning.

C. Use the idioms in your spoken or written answers to the following questions.

1. What are some causes that are pursued by *grass-roots* movements? Have you ever been a member of such an organization?

2. For what reasons do people *run for office?* Would you ever want to *toss your hat into the ring?* Why or why not?

3. If you were a politician, how would you feel about *pressing the flesh?* Why?

4. Have you ever had to deal with *red tape?* If so, explain what happened.

5. In what countries is the political atmosphere *right-wing?* In what countries is it *left-wing?* How would you characterize your own political philosophy?

D. Using the idioms from this unit or a previous one, develop a presentation about the political situation in a country you are familiar with. You may want to include the following:

- how politicians are selected;
- when the present leader of the country began serving in office;
- what the general political atmosphere is;
- what kinds of popular movements exist.

Unit 18
Control and Influence

run the show   to be responsible for all final decisions

USAGE NOTE: This idiom can be used in a negative sense when someone refuses to delegate decision-making responsibilities.

■ When committee members realized that organizing the convention was beyond their ability, a professional management firm was hired to **run the show.**

■ Don't ask *me* what to do about the scheduling problem. Mr. Tarketon is **running the show.**

run a tight ship   to manage in an efficient manner

■ The Wesley Plumbing Company is now a profitable one because Mrs. Wesley has been **running a tight ship** since her husband died.

■ Mr. Unger **runs a tight ship** in the classroom. All his students are attentive and obedient.

play favorites   to treat one person better than another person

GRAMMAR NOTE: The object form *favorites* is always plural.

■ A supervisor should never **play favorites** with office workers, or discontent will inevitably arise.

■ Johnny thought that his parents were **playing favorites** when they bought his sister a new bicycle.

in hand   under control

opposite meaning: **out of hand** (not under control)

■ The campers had the small brush fire **in hand** as fire crews arrived.

■ When an argument erupted between students from two rival schools, the situation soon got **out of hand.**

asleep at the wheel   not acting to control a situation properly

■ The company has suffered tremendous losses. It seems like the board of directors is **asleep at the wheel.**

■ Greg was fired because he wasn't monitoring the nuclear reactor control panel carefully enough. He was **asleep at the wheel,** as they say.

loose cannon   someone whose actions are unpredictable and uncontrolled
- The police officer with a history of complaints was removed from the force for being somewhat of a *loose cannon.*
- Don't let Mehmet convince you to join his crazy scheme. He's really a *loose cannon.*

pull (some) strings   to influence others for one's own advantage
USAGE NOTE: This idiom is used when someone is owed favors or has power over others.
- The dedicated soccer coach *pulled strings* in the club to get his practice field and time changed.
- Mr. Hansen has donated a lot of money to the private college, so he *pulled some strings* to get his daughter accepted this year.

throw one's weight around   to exert influence because of one's position or power
USAGE NOTE: This idiom is often used when someone exerts influence mainly to show that he or she has power over others.
- I detest working for our manager, Mr. Browbridge. He *throws his weight around* at every opportunity.
- If Ms. James has taken control of the matter, it must be a serious one. She's not someone who likes to *throw her weight around.*

be on the take   to accept one or more illegal payments
related idiom: **kickback** (illegal payments [noun])
USAGE NOTE: These idioms are often used for elected and appointed officials who accept bribes in exchange for favorable consideration.
- Why would city council members vote to increase trash collection fees over 50 percent if they weren't *on the take?*
- The crime organization required the store owner to pay a substantial *kickback* for protection services.

EXERCISES

A.   **Fill in each blank with the appropriate form of an idiom from this unit.**

1. The sheriff's deputy, who has a history of abusing his power, is considered somewhat of a _____ _____, even by his colleagues.

2. Our supervisor gives preferential treatment to employees who are most friendly to her. I don't think that she should _____ _____ like that.

3. Whenever an event or committee needs to be organized, Edward always volunteers to _____ _____ _____.

4. The neighbors had the small emergency _____ _____ by the time police arrived.

5. Once near bankruptcy, the ailing company has become profitable and efficient again, due in large part to a new chief executive officer who _____ _____ _____ _____.

6. How could you possibly have made that mistake? You must have been _____ _____ _____ _____.

7. The neighborhood bully scares away the other children because he's always trying to _____ _____ _____ _____.

(continued on next page)

8. The athletic coach had to _____ _____ _____ on campus to arrange a scholarship for the promising young volleyball player.

9. How could the Port Commission vote to turn over valuable land to the major industrial developer? Some members must _____ _____ _____ _____.

B. **Choose the statement in the right column that best responds to each question in the left column. Write the appropriate number in the blank.**

1. Have you heard that the governor has been charged with accepting kickbacks?

2. How did Cathy get so good at pulling strings to have her way?

3. How has the strike situation gotten so out of hand recently?

4. Do investigators finally have the recent string of deadly arson fires in hand?

5. Why is Supervisor Allen considered somewhat of a loose cannon?

____ a. They finally do because the FBI was brought in to run the show.

____ b. I'm not surprised. She's been accused of being on the take before.

____ c. Evidently it's because the union leaders don't run a tight ship.

____ d. When you've played favorites like she has, lots of people owe you favors.

____ e. Because he throws his weight around and forces people to go along with his crazy schemes.

C. **Use the idioms in your spoken or written answers to the following questions.**

1. Do you have your work or studies *in hand?* Is there any part of your life that you feel is getting *out of hand?* What is it?

2. What are some problems that result from *playing favorites?* Has this ever happened to you? Explain.

3. For what reasons might a teacher not *run a tight ship?*

4. What kind of personality might a *loose cannon* have? Do you know anyone like this?

5. Some people like to *run the show* and *throw their weight around.* Do you think that these people make good leaders? Why or why not?

D. **Using the idioms from this unit or a previous one, tell a classmate about who has the most and who has the least influence and control in your family. You may want to include the following:**

- how your parents treat you, your brothers, and sisters (as applicable);
- who makes most of the family decisions;
- who may not be in control of matters all the time;
- who makes an effort to control or influence others;
- who may sometimes behave strangely in your immediate or extended family.

Unit 19
Negotiation and Compromise

enter into   to begin serious discussion

USAGE NOTE: This idiom is followed by nouns such as *negotiations* or *talks*.

- The warring factions agreed to **enter into** negotiations toward a mediated settlement of their long-standing conflict.
- The couple **entered into** therapy because they couldn't resolve the problems in their relationship.

be on the table   to be open for consideration and negotiation

USAGE NOTE: The verb *put* can be used instead of *be*.

- All sections of the billion-dollar spending bill **were on the table** before the Senate subcommittee.
- At the meeting between opposing sides in the legal battle, both lawyers **put** all their demands **on the table.**

go-between   someone who serves as an intermediary between two opposing sides

USAGE NOTES: This idiom is used when opposing sides must negotiate through a third party. The verb *serve* is often used.

- The Swiss ambassador to Onglovia served as a **go-between** during negotiations to end civil unrest.
- When the Nottinghams had trouble communicating with their teen-age son, a school counselor agreed to be the **go-between.**

cut a deal   to negotiate an agreement
also: **hammer out**

GRAMMAR/USAGE NOTES: *Hammer out* is separable and is often followed by *an agreement.* It usually applies when it takes time to reach a consensus.

- We know we want to do business together, so let's **cut a deal** quickly, OK?
- It took three weeks for the Lifeguards' Association to **hammer out** an agreement with the city.

drive a hard bargain   to negotiate successfully without having to compromise

USAGE NOTE: This idiom is used when someone refuses to compromise in negotiations and still gets his or her own way.

- Are you saying that your asking price for the car is $14,000 and you won't lower the price under any circumstance? Boy, do you **drive a hard bargain!**
- Mr. Gunderson has acquired his millions partly by **driving a hard bargain** when he purchases new businesses.

break off   to discontinue, to suspend

GRAMMAR/USAGE NOTES: This idiom is usually used with nouns such as *talks* or *negotiations* and is not generally separated.

- After ten days of intense discussions, the opposing parties suddenly **broke off** talks.
- Negotiations were **broken off** when one side revealed sensitive details to the media.

meet halfway   to compromise with

GRAMMAR NOTE: This idiom is almost always separated.

- When parents and soccer players complained about excessive training and practices, the coach agreed to **meet** them **halfway.**
- I almost always agree to your plan of action, but this time I have some suggestions to make. Can't we **meet** each other **halfway** this one time?

give and take   cooperation through compromise

USAGE NOTE: This idiom is often preceded by *a matter of.*

- When asked how the complex bargaining had gone, the mediator replied, "It was simply a matter of **give and take.**"
- A relationship generally succeeds because each partner shares in a spirit of **give and take.**

happy medium   an appropriate balance

USAGE NOTES: This idiom is used when there is an excess of one action or condition over another. It often follows the verbs *arrive at* or *maintain.*

- The store clerk arrived at a **happy medium** with the owner over the frequency and length of her work breaks.
- Valerie used to put in sixty-hour weeks at the office, but now she maintains a **happy medium** between time at work and time with her family.

EXERCISES

A.   **Fill in each blank with the appropriate form of an idiom from this unit.**

To resolve a long-lasting labor strike, a local department store chain has

been forced to _____ _____ arbitration with the workers' union. A
                         1

_____ - _____ has already been selected to mediate a settlement.
      2

The strike began when chain management refused to _____
                                                          3

_____ _____ with union leaders, and now the chain has been hurt by a

tarnished reputation and declining sales. As a result, the union leadership sees

little reason to _____ the company _____ regarding the issues that
                      4

currently _____ _____ _____ _____.
               5

One of the most important issues involves achieving a _____ 6 _____ between benefits for part-time workers and those for regular salaried employees. The union is now in a position of strength and plans to _____ 7 _____ _____ _____ in the beginning of the talks. However, the real hope is that the wide discrepancy can be narrowed through a process of _____ _____ _____ 8 by both sides. It is also hoped that both sides will continue to negotiate and not _____ 9 _____ talks prematurely.

B. Choose the statement in the right column that best responds to each question in the left column. Write the appropriate number in the blank.

1. Is Sharon willing to meet her boss halfway over the salary matter?

2. Have the two companies finished negotiating a merger agreement?

3. Do you think that we can cut a deal by the end of the day?

4. Is a go-between still working to resolve differences between the warring countries?

5. Has a happy medium been reached between the soccer players and team owners?

____ a. Not yet. They haven't even decided what issues are to be on the table.

____ b. Not if you keep trying to drive such a hard bargain!

____ c. Yes. A U.N. envoy is working to prevent either side from breaking off talks.

____ d. Of course. She has always believed in give and take.

____ e. Yes, they've been able to hammer out an agreement before the tournament starts.

C. Use the idioms in your spoken or written answers to the following questions.

1. Must a marriage involve *give and take* between husband and wife in order to be successful? Why or why not?

2. Have you ever had to *meet* someone *halfway?* Explain what happened.

3. Do you feel comfortable *driving a hard bargain* on major purchases? Why or why not?

4. If you tried to *cut a deal* on a car purchase, what details would you discuss with the salesperson?

5. Have you achieved a *happy medium* between work and play in your life? Why or why not?

D. Using the idioms from this unit or a previous one, develop a dialogue or role play about two business executives discussing successful negotiations. You may want to include the following:

- what the negotiations are about;
- the people or businesses involved;
- the process of negotiating;
- the role of any intermediaries;
- the final outcome.

Unit 20
Promise and Commitment

give one's word   to make a promise

> GRAMMAR NOTE: This idiom may or may not be separated by an object.

- Terence *gave his word* that he'd serve as a volunteer at the charity auction event.
- Don't forget about starting your new weight-loss diet this weekend. You *gave* me *your word.*

keep one's word   to fulfill a promise
also: **make good on one's promise**
opposite meaning: **break one's word, go back on one's word**

- Did Brenda *keep her word* about coming to the birthday party?
- Olaf *made good on his promise* to graduate from high school and go to college.
- I'll be very disappointed if you *break your word* to me again.
- This is the third time that Brad has *gone back on his word.* Do you really think that he can be trusted?

cross one's heart (and hope to die)   to solemnly promise

> USAGE NOTE: This idiom can be used in a command form or with an understood "I."

- *Cross your heart* and tell me that you'll never sneak out of the house like that again.
- I didn't take any money from your wallet. *Cross my heart and hope to die.*

stick to   to follow, to obey, to adhere to

> USAGE NOTE: This idiom is often followed by the noun *word* or *promise.*

- If you *stick to* your word to give up cigarettes, soon you'll feel much better both physically and mentally.
- Manuel *stuck to* his promise to complete the drug rehabilitation program, and now he is leading a fulfilling life.

famous last words   a promise someone makes but no one expects him or her to keep

> USAGE NOTE: This idiom is often used alone in an exclamation.

- I just heard George declare again that he'll smoke his last cigar tonight. Those are *famous last words!*
- How many times have you sworn to avoid sweets altogether? *Famous last words!*

live up to   to meet a promise, standard, or expectation

- The new landlord *lived up to* her promise to make overdue improvements to the apartment complex.
- Darryl was never good at sports, so he couldn't *live up to* his father's dream that he would become a professional athlete.

follow through (on)   to fulfill or complete one's responsibilities
related form: **follow-through** (noun)

GRAMMAR NOTE: This idiom can be used either with or without an object and is separable.

- The police captain agreed to pursue the case seriously, and his detectives quickly *followed* it *through.*
- Kimberley *followed through on* her promise to check our house while we were away.
- The *follow-through* on the medical exam impressed the patient, who immediately received the proper medicine.

come through for   to do what someone has promised to another person

- Thanks for covering my job when I had to leave work early. You really *came through for* me.
- Doesn't it feel good to know that you have friends who will *come through for* you in any situation?

EXERCISES

A.   **Fill in each blank with the appropriate form of an idiom from this unit.**

1. I won't ever take money from your purse again without asking first, Mom. _____ _____ _____ and hope to die!

2. We didn't expect Henry to finish the long project without help, but to our surprise he _____ it _____ by himself.

3. Didn't you say that you weren't going to get so upset again? _____ _____ _____!

4. Even though Khaled has _____ _____ _____ not to eat so many sweets, his friends keep finding candy wrappers in his car.

5. Most voters were genuinely surprised when the president _____ _____ _____ his campaign promise to lower tax rates.

6. I really appreciated the fact that you _____ _____ _____ me on the Andujar account. I probably wouldn't have gotten it without your help.

7. Don't believe anything that Inez promises. She almost never _____ _____ _____.

8. If you _____ _____ a regular exercise schedule, you're bound to lose weight.

B. Choose the statement in the right column that best responds to each question in the left column. Write the appropriate number in the blank.

1. Has Ed ever gone back on his word about playing his music more softly?

2. Dad, cross my heart, I'll never be late coming home again, OK?

3. Has Michelle stuck to her pledge to give up dessert?

4. How do you know that your roommate will follow through for you?

5. Did your neighbors live up to their promise to feed your pets while you were gone?

____ a. I'd like to believe that, but I'm afraid those are just famous last words.

____ b. No, I'm glad to say he's kept his word so far.

____ c. Yes, this time they came through for me.

____ d. Unfortunately, she broke her word recently when she had pie at a restaurant.

____ e. Because I made him give his word several times that he would.

C. Use the idioms in your spoken or written answers to the following questions.

1. For what reasons might you *give your word* to someone?

2. What are some good reasons why you might *go back on your word?*

3. What kind of people are most likely to *follow through on* their responsibilities? Does this apply to you? Why or why not?

4. Was there ever a time when it was difficult to *stick to your word?* What happened?

5. Are there any common standards that all people of the world should *live up to?* Do you think that this will ever happen? Why or why not?

D. Using the idioms from this unit or a previous one, tell a classmate about an important promise that you once made. You may want to include the following:

- what the promise was;
- who you made the promise to and under what circumstances;
- the reaction of other people;
- how well you succeeded.

Review: Units 11–20

A. **Circle the expression that best completes each sentence.**

1. Do you mind if I wait until next week to _____ the money I owe?
   a. chip in
   b. pay back
   c. put aside

2. Mismanagement and declining profits caused the company to _____ several hundred workers.
   a. lay off
   b. put in for
   c. hammer out

3. Concerned citizens formed a _____ movement to abolish the unfair law.
   a. thin-skinned
   b. soft-hearted
   c. grass-roots

4. The traffic was _____ on my way to work because of an accident on the freeway.
   a. up to speed
   b. stop-and-go
   c. give and take

5. Sometimes Terry is such an unpleasant person. How can you _____ her so well?
   a. get along with
   b. hit it off
   c. wrap up

6. If Janine _____ that she'd do it for you, then you can be sure that she will.
   a. met you halfway
   b. played favorites
   c. gave her word

7. My life seems to be _____ these days. Nothing interesting is happening.
   a. in a rut
   b. on the rocks
   c. asleep at the wheel

8. Yolanda's daughter must have inherited her energetic character. She's pretty much a _____ most of the time.
   a. stick in the mud
   b. live wire
   c. couch potato

9. Curt will never let you share in the decision making. He expects to _____.
   a. run the show
   b. pull strings
   c. be on the take

10. The executives agreed to _____ negotiations about a merger between their two companies.
    a. do business with
    b. come through for
    c. enter into

B. **Indicate whether each statement is TRUE (T) or FALSE (F).**

_____ 1. Traffic might be backed up because of a fender bender.
_____ 2. A hot-headed person always has his or her emotions in hand.
_____ 3. If you're part of today's rat race, then you're probably always on the go.
_____ 4. If you cut a deal quickly, then you had to deal with a lot of red tape.
_____ 5. A food company that is a household word would have a lot of products on the market.
_____ 6. Someone who is running for office has already been sworn in.
_____ 7. If you lived up to your responsibilities, you would go back on your word.
_____ 8. You'd buy something on credit if you had laid aside enough cash to pay for it.
_____ 9. A tough cookie might be someone who runs a tight ship.
_____ 10. It would be out of character for a soft-hearted person to drive a hard bargain.

C. Complete the puzzle with the missing parts of the idioms in the sentences below.

ACROSS

1. The workers went on _____ for better pay.
3. I made out a _____ to pay for the purchase.
5. We arrived at a happy _____ about TV viewing.
8. The politician took _____ on January 1.
9. It's Monday. Back to the _____ .
12. Her views are definitely not _____-of-the-road.
14. Let's meet and discuss it _____ to face.
15. She's got a good head on her _____ .
18. You're quitting tobacco? _____ last words!
19. Most people love the _____ comforts of home.

DOWN

1. Traffic was up to _____ past the accident scene.
2. The store went out of _____ due to the economy.
4. It's out of _____ for Leanne to shout.
6. A go-_____ was assigned to mediate the case.
7. Stay away from Lou. He's a loose _____ .
10. Could I borrow two _____ to use the pay phone?
11. I'd like to escape this dog-eat-dog _____ .
13. Did she make good on her _____ to meet you?
16. Is Matt _____ in the head or just slow to react?
17. Quiet the children down. They're out of _____.

Unit 21
Feelings and Reactions

open up   to express or reveal one's true emotions or thoughts

GRAMMAR/USAGE NOTES: *Open up* is intransitive. It is often followed by the prepositions *about* and *to.*

- The psychologist had a hard time getting the reluctant client to **open up** about her childhood memories.
- Instead of holding in your feelings, why don't you **open up** to me and share them?

get off one's chest   to express one's true thoughts or feelings after a long period of time

GRAMMAR NOTE: An object must follow the verb *get.*

- After years of keeping her life-long secret from her family, Miriam felt good **getting** the truth **off her chest.**
- Mr. Inez had never complained to his boss about his poor salary, but he finally decided to **get** it **off his chest.**

pour out   to reveal what is troubling someone, to allow to flow

GRAMMAR/USAGE NOTES: This idiom is separable and is usually used with one of the following nouns as the object: *heart, grief, sorrow,* or *feelings.*

- I could tell that Casey had been holding his feelings in for a long time when he **poured** his heart **out** to me over the phone.
- The relatives of the deceased woman **poured out** their grief at the memorial service.

break out in(to) laughter/tears   to laugh or cry suddenly
also: **burst out in(to) laughter/tears**

USAGE NOTE: An adverb such as *suddenly* can be used, even though it repeats the meaning of the idiom.

- The room was relatively quiet until a group of people in the back **broke out in laughter.**
- First the boy's lips quivered, then his eyes watered, and suddenly he **burst out into tears.**

choke up   to be overcome with emotion and be unable to speak

GRAMMAR/USAGE NOTES: This idiom can be used with an object, in which case it should be separated. It is also commonly used in passive form with *all.*

- The retiring vice-president **choked up** while delivering his farewell speech to colleagues.
- Whenever I talk about my Mom's struggle with chronic arthritis, it **chokes** me **up.**
- Carl was all **choked up** when his friends came to his parent's funeral.

get to   to affect emotionally
- Mr. Robertson let his son's sarcastic comments *get to* him and reacted angrily.
- Stella is deliberately provoking you when she says things like that. Try not to let it *get to* you.

break someone's heart   to injure someone's feelings greatly
- It would *break my heart* if any members of my family moved far away.
- When Angela told Tony that their engagement was over, it nearly *broke Tony's heart.*

burst someone's bubble   to disappoint by correcting someone's mistaken impression
- I hate to be the one to *burst your bubble,* but your school's team didn't win last night. It lost!
- The popular teacher *burst everyone's bubble* by being arrested for the petty crime of shoplifting.

be music to someone's ears   to be good news or information to someone
- When the coach told the players that tomorrow's practice was canceled, it *was music to their ears.*
- Did you suggest eating out tonight instead of cooking? That's *music to my ears!*

hard pill to swallow   some news or information that is very difficult to accept
GRAMMAR/USAGE NOTES: The idiom is usually separated by a prepositional phrase starting with *for,* which names a person. The adjective *bitter* can be used instead of *hard.*
- News of my rejection for the executive position in marketing was a *hard pill* for me *to swallow.*
- Learning that he would rarely get to see his children was a *bitter pill* for the convicted felon *to swallow.*

EXERCISES

A.   Fill in each blank with the appropriate form of an idiom from this unit. Some sentences may have more than one correct answer.

LONI: Hi, Inge. Your eyes are misty! You look like you're about to _____ _____
      $\underset{1}{}$
      _____ _____.

INGE: I am, Loni. My boyfriend, Luke, just _____ _____ _____ by telling
      $\underset{2}{}$
      me that our relationship was over. I can't believe it.

LONI: Wow, I can understand how that would really _____ _____ you. You
      $\underset{3}{}$
      must be miserable.

INGE: I am. I always expected that we would get married some day. Boy, did Luke
      _____ _____ _____ big time!
      $\underset{4}{}$

LONI: Rejection is always a _____ _____ _____ _____. I've been
      $\underset{5}{}$
      through it myself.

INGE: Really? After it happened, did you have someone to _____ _____ to,
      $\underset{6}{}$
      or did you keep it to yourself?

LONI: At first I didn't talk to anyone, but finally my best friend asked me what the

matter was. I was so _____ _____ at first that the words wouldn't come
            7

out. Finally the words flowed and I _____ it all _____ _____
                                            8

_____.

INGE: I bet that felt good. It must be therapeutic to _____ _____ one's feelings
                                                              9

to a friend.

LONI: So why don't you tell me what happened? Maybe I can give you some helpful

advice.

INGE: Oh, thank you. That _____ _____ _____ _____ _____!
                                  10

I'd love to.

B. **Choose the statement in the right column that best responds to each question in the left column. Write the appropriate number in the blank.**

1. Did the sad movie ending really get to you?

2. Why does Nancy look like she's about to burst out in tears?

3. Does Jack have anyone to open up to about his divorce?

4. I hate to burst your bubble, but isn't 58% a failing grade, not a passing one?

5. Have you heard that Grace broke your ex-husband's heart?

____ a. That's music to my ears! Finally I get some revenge.

____ b. Yes, I was all choked up as I left the theater.

____ c. I don't know, but she must have something to get off her chest.

____ d. He's been pouring his feelings out to a counselor.

____ e. Oh, no, you're right! That's a hard pill to swallow right now.

C. **Use the idioms in your spoken or written answers to the following questions.**

1. What kinds of things make you *break out in laughter* or *burst out in tears?*

2. What occupations involve listening to people *pour out* their feelings? Would you be interested in such a job? Why or why not?

3. What are some actions or statements that could *break your heart?* Have you ever *broken someone's heart?* What happened?

4. Has anything happened in your life that was a *bitter pill to swallow?* What was it?

5. What kinds of feelings might you have if you were *all choked up?*

D. **Using the idioms from this unit or a previous one, tell a classmate about how you express your feelings. You may want to include the following:**

- what situations affect you emotionally;
- who you best express your feelings to;
- why you're quick or slow to laugh or cry;
- what someone has done to disappoint you;
- what good news you've had recently.

Unit 22
Enthusiasm and Indifference

be crazy about   to be very interested in or overly enthusiastic about
also: **be nuts about**

USAGE NOTE: A gerund (verb + -*ing*) often follows these idioms.

- Joseph *is crazy about* old movies from the forties and fifties. Sometimes he stays up all night watching them.
- Some people *are* so *nuts about* riding on the largest rollercoasters in the world that they spend each vacation visiting different ones.

get into the spirit   to become enthusiastic about something

USAGE NOTE: This idiom can be used when there's been some delay in becoming enthusiastic.

- There wasn't much fan support until the second half of the game, when a touchdown for the home team really *got* the crowd *into the spirit.*
- The Christmas season is when many people *get into the spirit* of gift-giving.

pump up   to excite, to fill with enthusiasm
also: **fire up**

GRAMMAR NOTE: These idioms are separable.

- The roar of the crowd *pumped up* the batter, who sent the ball into the upper bleachers for a home run.
- You could tell that the runners were *fired up* for the 400-meter run by how they were poised at the starting line.

liven up   to make or become more lively or active

GRAMMAR/USAGE NOTES: This idiom is used with or without an object. When an object is used, it is separable. The noun *party* is often used as the object.

- Onlookers at the beach volleyball match *livened up* when they heard there would be an amateur match for prizes.
- We need different music to *liven* the party *up*. Where's that new Art Medina CD?

throw cold water on   to dampen enthusiasm for, to discourage interest in
also: **throw a wet blanket on**

- I hate to be the one to *throw cold water on* your plans, but don't you realize how impractical they are?
- My parents *threw a wet blanket on* my plans to have a party while they were gone.

it's all the same to   a phrase used to indicate indifference toward something

USAGE NOTE: The person who is indifferent is mentioned after *to*.

- If *it's all the same to* you, I'd rather go to bed early tonight than stay up and watch TV.
- *It's all the same to* Jeff if you stay in our guest bedroom instead of staying in a motel.

not give a darn   to be indifferent, not to have any care or concern at all

also: **not give a hoot**

- Amber's grades are so bad because she does*n't give a darn* about school or the future. She only lives for the moment.
- This small island is such a boring place for our vacation that I do*n't give a hoot* what you have planned for us.

go with the crowd   to choose to do or think the same as others

- The lone juror who thought that the defendant might be innocent decided to *go with the crowd* and vote for a conviction anyway.
- Jack never likes to take a leading role in any affair. He's happy just *going with the crowd.*

might as well   for no particular reason, as an alternative

GRAMMAR NOTE: This idiom is used as an auxiliary form before the verb.

- I'm not ready to go yet so you *might as well* leave without me. I'll see you there.
- Since it's too wet outside to play softball, we *might as well* play cards inside.

EXERCISES

A.   **Fill in each blank with the appropriate form of an idiom from this unit. Some sentences may have more than one correct answer.**

1. The people in the crowd gathered in front of the amusement park entrance were all _____ _____ for the moment when they could rush in.

2. The guests are starting to act bored. Is there any music to _____ _____ the party?

3. Well, it's getting late, and there's nothing on TV, so we _____ _____ _____ go to bed.

4. The teenager next door comes and goes as he pleases because his parents do _____ _____ _____ _____ about his whereabouts.

5. I don't want to _____ _____ _____ _____ your plan, but do you have any idea how expensive a two-week cruise can be?

6. If _____ _____ _____ _____ _____ you, it would be better to postpone our drive in the country until next weekend.

7. With their children grown up and away at school, it was difficult for the Carmichaels to _____ _____ _____ _____ of Thanksgiving.

8. Is that another big box of chocolates you're eating? You really _____ _____ _____ sweet things, aren't you?

9. Don't look to me for a decision. This time I'm just _____ _____ _____ _____.

B. Choose the statement in the right column that best responds to each question in the left column. Write the appropriate number in the blank.

1. Why are so many people nuts about that popular TV program?

2. If it's all the same to you, can we eat out tomorrow night instead of tonight?

3. Why isn't the crowd getting into the spirit of the game?

4. What could we do to liven up the school talent show this year?

5. Why is Ben the only one who's crazy about visiting the museum again?

____ a. Fine. We might as well have leftovers this evening.

____ b. We could fire up the students to get more actively involved.

____ c. I have no idea. I really don't give a darn about TV at all.

____ d. I don't know. He's usually one to just go with the crowd.

____ e. The bad weather has thrown cold water on everyone's team spirit.

C. Use the idioms in your spoken or written answers to the following questions.

1. What are some activities you could plan that would *liven up* a party?

2. If you were about to play a professional sport such as soccer or football, how would you *pump* yourself *up?*

3. Is there anything in life that you *are crazy about?* What is it?

4. Is there anything you do*n't give a hoot about?* What is it?

5. What are some reasons why you might not *go with the crowd* in a given situation?

D. Using the idioms from this unit or a previous one, develop a dialogue or role play about generating enthusiasm among your friends, some of whom are couch potatoes, for an activity. You may want to include the following:

- what the activity is;
- how you try to generate enthusiasm among your friends;
- who becomes enthusiastic;
- who is willing to agree to anything, doesn't care, or is indifferent;
- whether anyone tries to discourage interest in the activity.

Unit 23
Surprise and Shock

take by surprise to surprise someone

GRAMMAR NOTE: An object follows the verb *take*.

- The company's sudden announcement that it was going bankrupt *took* everybody *by surprise.*
- Oh! I didn't hear you coming up the steps. You *took* me *by surprise.*

give someone a start to startle someone

USAGE NOTE: The adverb *quite* can be added before the article *a*.

- Don't sneak up on me like that. You *gave* me *a start.*
- A sudden noise behind him on the isolated park trail *gave* Doug quite *a start.*

take aback to surprise, to shock

GRAMMAR/USAGE NOTES: This idiom is separable and usually occurs in passive form. It is used when someone is surprised by unexpected news.

- It really *takes* me *aback* that you lied about the accident. It was only partly your fault anyway.
- Deborah's parents were *taken aback* by their daughter's news that she was joining an expedition to climb Mt. Everest.

throw for a loop to do or say something that others would never expect

GRAMMAR NOTE: An object follows the verb *throw*.

- I've rarely seen my boss lose his temper, and when he does, it always *throws* me *for a loop.*
- Guillermo, the most trusted man in the department, *threw* everyone *for a loop* when he stole several thousand dollars and disappeared.

heart-stopper something that causes great surprise or shock

- News of the rock star's medical emergency on stage was a real *heart-stopper* to all her fans.
- It was a *heart-stopper* when Jerry's long-lost brother appeared at the door after a twenty-year absence.

71

what on earth   an expression of disbelief
also: **what in the world, what the devil**

GRAMMAR NOTE: These idioms are used alone with a question mark or to begin a sentence in question form.

- *What on earth?* Did you just see that strange plane fly by?
- *What in the world* are you doing asleep on the couch at 2:00 A.M.?
- *What the devil* was that? You'd better check the backyard.

drop a bombshell   to announce shocking news

- Roberto *dropped a bombshell* when he told his family of his plans to enter the ministry.
- The recently appointed deputy mayor *dropped a bombshell* when she announced an early retirement.

turn over in one's grave   to be shocked beyond belief

GRAMMAR/USAGE NOTES: The subject is the deceased person who would be shocked if he or she knew a certain thing.

- Grandpa Bob would *turn over in his grave* if he saw how his relatives were spending their inheritance.

EXERCISES

A. Fill in each blank with the appropriate form of an idiom from this unit. Some sentences may have more than one correct answer.

ANN: _____ _____ _____? Did you feel that, Dad?
              ¹

DAD: I sure did. The whole room shook. It _____ _____ quite _____
                                               ²

_____ .

ANN: Was it an earthquake?

DAD: I guess so! It's been a long time since the last one struck.

ANN: Yeah, that's why this one _____ us _____ _____ _____ at first. It
                                         ³

was a _____ - _____ for me, that's for sure.
                ⁴

DAD: Some day a really big one will strike. You know, around 8.0 on the Richter scale.

ANN: Funny you should mention the big one. Please sit down—I'm going to

_____ _____ _____ on you right now, Dad.
  ⁵

DAD: A bombshell? What do you mean?

ANN: Well, I've decided to move out of the house and into my own apartment.

DAD: What? Your mother would _____ _____ _____ _____ _____
                                    ⁶

if she could hear you say that, Ann. And that announcement really _____
                                               ⁷

me _____ _____ too! Why, Ann?

ANN: I knew that you would be _____ _____ like this. I'm sorry, Dad, but it's
                                    ⁸

time for me to be on my own.

DAD: I respect that. It's just that this house is too big for only one person. It will feel very empty without you around.

ANN: I'm sorry, Dad. But I'll still spend plenty of time here!

B. **Choose the statement in the right column that best responds to each question in the left column. Write the appropriate number in the blank.**

1. You've broken your leg! What in the world happened?
2. What on earth could that strange noise be?
3. Oh, you gave me such a start. Why are you sitting in the dark like that?
4. Wouldn't news of the royal couple's divorce be a real heart-stopper?
5. Hasn't news of Mr. Sorenson's arrest for embezzlement thrown everyone for a loop?

____ a. A tree took me by surprise while I was skiing.
____ b. Yes. I'm sure his mother is turning over in her grave.
____ c. Yes, if they announced it, they would be dropping a bombshell.
____ d. I'm meditating. I'm sorry that you were taken aback.
____ e. I don't know. And what the devil could that strange smell be?

C. **Use the idioms in your spoken or written answers to the following questions.**

1. What could someone in your family do that might cause your ancestors to **turn over in their graves?**
2. What dangerous or thrilling activity might be considered a **heart-stopper?**
3. Has a friend or family member ever **thrown** you **for a loop?** What did he or she say?
4. How could you **give someone a start?** Has this happened to you recently?
5. If a politician went public to **drop a bombshell,** what might it be about?

D. **Using the idioms from this unit or a previous one, develop a dialogue or role play about two family members who are shocked by some news. You may want to include the following:**

- what surprises or shocks them;
- why it surprises them;
- who else is also shocked;
- what aspect of the event is completely unexpected to them.

Unit 24
Humor and Seriousness

tickle someone's funny bone   to amuse someone, to make someone laugh
- The joke about the hungry rabbit *tickled my funny bone.*
- It *tickled Rick's funny bone* to hear his friend's imitation of his donkey-like laugh.

crack up   to laugh loudly; to cause to laugh loudly
GRAMMAR NOTES: This idiom may be used with or without an object, and can it be transitive or intransitive. When an object is used, it is separable.
- The nightclub audience *cracked up* at the comedian's constant stream of jokes.
- It always *cracks* me *up* when someone mispronounces my last name badly. I've heard it pronounced so many different ways.

double up   to laugh so hard that someone almost feels pain
also: **tie up in knots**

GRAMMAR/USAGE NOTES: *Double up* is usually intransitive, followed by the phrase *in laughter. Tie up in knots* is usually transitive, separated by an object.
- The classroom *doubled up* in laughter when the teacher tripped over a chair and fell.
- The hilarious hour-long comedy special on TV *tied* us *up in knots* the whole time.

for laughs   for the sole purpose of having fun
USAGE NOTE: The adverb *just* can be added before this idiom.
- Hey, *for laughs* why don't we enter that fun run in the park tomorrow?
- We went on the Killer Thriller rollercoaster five times in a row just *for laughs.*

lighten up   to add humor to an otherwise serious situation, to make or become less serious
GRAMMAR/USAGE NOTES: This idiom is used with or without an object and is separable. The object *things* is often used.
- I wish Mark would *lighten up* a little. He takes things too seriously sometimes.
- Janus tried to *lighten* things *up* at the reception by playing a dance tune on the piano.

keep a straight face   to try to show no emotion when one is really laughing inside
- It was hard for me to *keep a straight face* when I told Ed I'd be out of town the night of his birthday, because I knew his friends had planned a surprise party.

74

no laughing matter   a matter to be taken seriously

    GRAMMAR NOTE: The noun *matter* cannot be made plural.

- A burglary in our neighborhood is *no laughing matter.* We'll have to be more careful about security.
- It was *no laughing matter* when Lauren got her third ticket for speeding.

mean business   to be serious about a situation

- Father is on his way upstairs to talk to you, and he looks like he *means business.*
- Are you just joking about our starting a software company together, or do you *mean business?*

hit home   to make a serious impression on someone

- The importance of taking care of herself really *hit home* for Chris when her doctor told her that her weight was causing serious problems.
- The downturn in the economy has really *hit home* at our firm. Recently there were ten more layoffs.

EXERCISES

A.   **Fill in each blank with the appropriate form of an idiom from this unit.**

1. Why don't we watch old family movies from ten years ago just _____ _____?

2. I can't explain why that ridiculous joke still _____ _____ _____ _____.

3. This time the baby-sitter didn't fool around about punishing the boys when they misbehaved. She showed them that she _____ _____ by sending them to their rooms.

4. The documentary about teenage runaways really _____ _____ for the teenager who had been feeling sorry for herself.

5. Getting arrested for writing graffiti on the walls of public buildings is _____ _____ _____.

6. Martha tried to _____ _____ _____ _____ when she lied to Steve about a surprise party for him.

7. Ursula was rolling on the floor in apparent pain from being _____ _____ in laughter.

8. Everyone was so serious at the farewell party for our boss. The host tried to _____ things _____ with charades, but no one was in the mood.

9. Everyone in the audience _____ _____ when the elderly comedian joked about how difficult romance was for him.

B. Choose the statement in the right column that best responds to each question in the left column. Write the appropriate number in the blank.

1. Have you ever found yourself tied up in knots in a public place?

2. Does Janet always try to keep a straight face like that?

3. Do you think that Dad means business about quitting his job and starting his own company?

4. Why did Bradley crack up in the middle of the principal's speech?

5. What would you like to do for laughs this weekend?

____ a. Well, I'm sure we'd be doubled up in laughter if we went to a comedy club.

____ b. Right now he does. When the consequences hit home, he'll reconsider.

____ c. Yes, unfortunately. I wish she'd lighten up more.

____ d. Yes, once something tickled my funny bone in court.

____ e. I don't know, but it was no laughing matter to the principal.

C. Use the idioms in your spoken or written answers to the following questions.

1. What tone of voice and facial expression would you have if you *meant business?* Have you ever had to act this way? Explain.

2. What could you do to help a serious friend *lighten up?*

3. What problem in the world is *no laughing matter* to you? What should be done about it?

4. When have you had trouble *keeping a straight face?*

5. What comedians or comedy shows on TV *crack* you *up?*

D. Using the idioms from this unit or a previous one, tell a classmate about things that you find humorous. You may want to include the following:

- what you do for fun;
- how skilled you are at telling jokes;
- what your favorite joke is;
- what other people do that amuses you;
- things that are not so humorous; things that you take seriously.

Unit 25
Embarrassment and Sympathy

on the spot   in an awkward position that could cause embarrassment

USAGE NOTE: The verbs *be, feel,* and *put* are commonly used.

- The prosecuting attorney put the witness **on the spot** about his testimony.
- Sue felt **on the spot** when a TV crew stopped her on the street to ask a question.

red-faced   visibly embarrassed

- The teenage girl with the bulging backpack became **red-faced** when the alarm system at the public library went off.
- The waiter became **red-faced** when he realized that customers were laughing at a piece of food on his face.

one's ears burn   to be very embarrassed

GRAMMAR/USAGE NOTES: This idiom is often used in present or past progressive form. Its usage reflects the fact that the ears get red and feel hot when one is very embarrassed.

- That was an embarrassing story you told about me at the party. Couldn't you see that *my ears were burning?*
- *Isaac's ears burned* as he was criticized for not playing well during the game.

save face   to preserve one's dignity or image

- In a situation where one's guilt is obvious, it's better to **save face** by admitting responsibility and offering compensation.
- The player who had almost lost a semifinal game for our team **saved face** by scoring two goals in the championship match.

live down   to recover one's dignity after an embarrassing or disgraceful situation

USAGE NOTE: The negative forms *never* and *not* are often used.

- Upon release from state prison, the ex-convict moved to a small town and tried to *live down* his past.
- Clay has *never* been able to *live down* the time that friends heard him talking in his sleep.

feel sorry for   to pity, to have sympathy for
also: **take pity on**

- I don't think Michael's to blame for most of his problems, so I *feel* really *sorry for* him.
- Mrs. Lewis *takes pity on* every person she sees begging for money and gives each a dollar.

one's heart goes out to   one expresses great sympathy for another person's misfortune

GRAMMAR NOTE: The noun *heart* can be made plural.

- In my card to Paul after his dad's funeral, I wrote, *"My heart goes out to* you and your family during this difficult time."
- Every winter, *our hearts go out to* the countless unfortunate people who have no food or shelter for the night.

a shoulder to cry on   someone who offers consolation and advice

USAGE NOTE: This idiom is often used with the verbs *need* or *offer*.

- If you ever need *a shoulder to cry on*, you can always count on me.
- My mom offered me *a shoulder to cry on* when I was having difficulty with my girlfriend.

have a heart   to be kinder, to be more sympathetic

GRAMMAR NOTE: This idiom is used in a direct or indirect command form.

- I asked the policeman to *have a heart* and not ticket me for speeding to the hospital for the birth of my child.
- Please don't give us too much homework over the holiday, professor. *Have a heart!*

EXERCISES

 A.   Fill in each blank with the appropriate form of an idiom from this unit. Some sentences may have more than one correct answer.

1. Our football team is losing 21-0. The best way that it can _____ _____ is by scoring at least one goal.

2. Mom, don't make me do the yard work on the same day that my friends have planned a picnic. Come on, _____ _____ _____!

3. I couldn't believe how _____ -_____ Nathan got when he told me about the dent he put in my new car.

4. Gail was put _____ _____ _____ when the teacher asked her a simple question in front of the class, and she didn't know the answer.

5. I'm always available if you ever have a serious problem and need _____ _____ _____ _____ _____.

6. When Terry lost a close friend, I wrote her a note that said, "_____ _____ _____ _____ _____ you for your personal loss."

7. Isn't David unfortunate to have parents who don't seem to care about him? That's why I really _____ _____ _____ him.

8. I felt really embarrassed when I spilled my coffee all over the classroom carpet. Did you notice that _____ _____ _____ _____?

9. Ever since Martin accidentally used our old boss's name while introducing the new boss to the office staff, he's been trying to _____ it _____.

B. Choose the statement in the right column that best responds to each question in the left column. Write the appropriate number in the blank.

1. Kim's problem is her own fault. Why should I take pity on her?

2. Did Mr. Thomas try to save face by giving back the money he stole?

3. Why do you feel sorry for Michael so often?

4. Did you feel on the spot when you had to talk to the group unexpectedly?

5. Did you offer your neighbor a shoulder to cry on after her difficult divorce?

_____ a. Yes, but he'll never be able to live down committing the crime.

_____ b. Because he's clumsy and turns red-faced whenever he's spoken to.

_____ c. Because she's just a teenager. Come on, have a heart!

_____ d. Yes. My heart went out to her because I knew what she was feeling.

_____ e. Of course. And my ears were burning because I didn't know what to say!

C. Use the idioms in your spoken or written answers to the following questions.

1. What are some common things that cause people to become *red-faced?* When was the last time that this happened to you?

2. What could you do to hide the fact that *your ears were burning?*

3. Have you ever offered anyone *a shoulder to cry on?* What happened?

4. What serious mistake or crime would be difficult for someone to *live down?*

5. Give an example of a situation where you might feel that you had to *save face.*

D. Using the idioms from this unit or a previous one, develop a dialogue or role play about a time when you got embarrassed and needed sympathy from your friends. You may want to include the following:

- how the awkward situation embarrassed you;
- how you expressed your embarrassment;
- whether your pride was involved;
- who had sympathy for you.

Unit 26
Pride and Ego

take pride in   to be proud of
- You can see how the Teasleys *take pride in* their home by the way they care for the front yard.
- You can *take pride in* your accomplishments if you always do your very best.

one's pride and joy   something that one is very proud of
also: **the apple of one's eye**

USAGE NOTES: *The apple of one's eye* refers to people. *One's pride and joy* can be a person or a thing.
- That beautiful sculpture in the corner is *his pride and joy.* He doesn't like anyone to touch it.
- Six-year-old Lynette is *the apple of her father's eye.* He gives her everything she wants.

hold one's head high   to remain proud or strong even when it is difficult to do so
also: **keep one's chin up**
- The accused woman *held her head high* and proclaimed her innocence to the judge and the jury.
- Just when you think things can't get worse, they do. Then it's time to really *keep your chin up.*

blow one's own horn   to praise oneself, to brag about one's accomplishments
also: **toot one's own horn**
- Warren gets more Employee of the Month awards than the rest of us because he's always *blowing his own horn* around his boss.
- If you don't mind my *tooting my own horn*, I just got that important promotion I was hoping for.

be stuck up   to be filled with self-importance, to be arrogant
also: **have a big head**
USAGE NOTES: The verb *act* can be used instead of *be* in *be stuck up*. This idiom is used when someone ignores other people because of an apparent feeling of superiority.
- The new girl in school *was stuck up* for weeks, but finally she made friends with others.
- Why does Jerry *act stuck up* only when he's among strangers?
- When I first met Bruce he seemed to *have a big head,* but soon I realized it was not intentional.

80

steal the show   to be the most important part of some activity or situation

- The elephants and monkeys at a circus are always fun, but the lions *steal the show.*
- The main guests on the talk show were a famous politician and actress, but it was a Japanese sushi chef demonstrating his amazing skills who *stole the show.*

take a back seat (to)   to remain in the background while someone else receives attention

- Dr. Bettner always *took a back seat* and let his associate report the results of their medical research to the press.
- As one of the president's newest cabinet members, Helena Davis had no intention of *taking a back seat to* the more senior members.

hurt someone's feelings   to affect someone's pride or self-image negatively

GRAMMAR NOTE: The word *feelings* is always plural.

- His lack of concern for me really *hurts my feelings.* I thought we were best friends.
- It would *hurt his feelings* if he knew you thought his team would lose the next game.

EXERCISES

A.   Fill in each blank with the appropriate form of an idiom from this unit. Some sentences may have more than one correct answer.

JAY: Oh, look, there's Matt driving his restored 1956 Chevy Bel Air.

LISA: Wow, it's all polished and shiny. He must really _____ _____ _____
       1
       his car.

JAY: He does. He's poured a lot of money into restoring it. It's clearly _____
       2
       _____ _____ _____.

LISA: It's funny—I like Matt now, but in the beginning I didn't.

JAY: Oh, what do you mean?

LISA: When he first transferred to our school, he _____ _____
       3
       _____—you know, he wouldn't talk to others.

JAY: Yeah, and I remember that he _____ _____ _____ in the first
       4
       football game he played. He made three touchdowns in the first half.

LISA: I bet no one else has ever done that at our school!

JAY: I don't mean to _____ _____ _____ _____, but I once scored
       5
       three touchdowns in a game too!

LISA: Yeah, but not in one half.

JAY: Gee, thanks, Lisa. Now you've _____ _____ _____!
       6

LISA: Oh, I'm sorry. I know you've _____ _____ _____ _____
       7
       _____ Matt ever since he joined the team.

(continued on next page)

JAY: Yeah, now Matt is the school football star. Frankly, I'm getting tired of it.

LISA: Don't be jealous. Matt will never have the grade point average you do, so you

can still _____ _____ _____ _____. And besides, you have
$\quad\quad\quad\quad\quad\quad_{8}$

something else that Matt never will.

JAY: What's that?

LISA: A great friend like me!

B.   **Choose the statement in the right column that best responds to each question in the left column. Write the appropriate number in the blank.**

1. Why does it seem that Kevin is always tooting his own horn?

2. Is two-year-old Johnny the apple of his mother's eye?

3. Didn't Betty hurt your feelings when she commented on your old clothes?

4. Don't you mind taking a back seat to Marsha all the time?

5. Why doesn't Ms. Hansen take more pride in her accomplishments?

____ a. No, people like her just like to blow their own horn. I don't let it affect me.

____ b. Maybe it's because he has such a big head.

____ c. Yes, he's so cute that he's always stealing the show.

____ d. Not really. I just kept my chin up and ignored what she said.

____ e. I don't know. I guess she has so many problems that it's hard for her to hold her head high.

C.   **Use the idioms in your spoken or written answers to the following questions.**

1. What should you do if you have **hurt someone's feelings?**

2. Why do some people prefer to **take a back seat,** while other people prefer to **steal the show?** Which is true for you? Give an example, if possible.

3. What are some typical actions of someone who **has a big head?**

4. Are you willing to **toot your own horn** by telling about one of your most special accomplishments?

5. What possession do you consider **your pride and joy?**

D.   **Using the idioms from this unit or a previous one, develop a presentation about an imaginary time when you did something very special. You may want to include the following:**

- how the special thing made you feel;
- how important your role was;
- how you bragged about it;
- whether anyone criticized you.

Unit 27
Arguing and Complaining

have words (with)   to argue (with)
- Two angry motorists *had words* at an intersection before they drove on.
- I didn't want to *have words with* my boss, but when he insulted me again, I had to say something.

have it out with   to finally have a serious argument or discussion with
GRAMMAR NOTE: Only the pronoun *it* can be used after the verb.
- One of these days we'll *have it out with* the neighbor who keeps playing loud music late at night.
- It was good that we finally *had it out with* each other. Now we can try to solve our problems.

split hairs   to argue in a very particular, even unreasonable, way
also: **nitpick**
GRAMMAR NOTE: *Nitpick* is sometimes spelled as two words.
- Do you always have to *split hairs* when we argue? Everything's a fine point to you!
- Why don't you stop *nitpicking* over the error of 50 cents on your bank statement? You've been going over the numbers for hours.

make a big deal of   to exaggerate the importance or impact of a problem
also: **make an issue of, make a fuss of**
GRAMMAR/USAGE NOTES: The adverb *such* is often added before the indefinite article, and *of* can be substituted with *about*.
- Don't *make* such *a big deal of* the broken window. The children didn't mean to do it.
- *Making an issue of* my weight is not going to help me lose the few pounds I still need to shed.
- What on earth are you *making* such *a fuss about?* Calm down and relax!

harp on   to discuss an issue repeatedly
- Antoine finally rented his own apartment because he couldn't stand listening to his parents *harp on* his unwillingness to help around the house.
- I'll just resent you further if you continue to *harp on* my sleeping habits. I'll go to sleep and get up when I want!

rant and rave　　to continue an almost violent verbal attack on someone

GRAMMAR/USAGE NOTES: This idiom is intransitive. It is often followed by the preposition *at*.

- The neighbors were *ranting and raving* about some domestic problem all afternoon.
- If you continue to *rant and rave* at me like this, I'll just leave the room.

have an ax to grind　　to have a personal reason for complaining or taking action

- The store clerk *had an ax to grind* about working long hours without extra pay.
- Evidently, the arsonist *had an ax to grind* when he set fire to his former apartment building after being evicted.

cause a stir　　to cause a greater reaction than was thought possible
also: **stir up a hornet's nest**

USAGE NOTE: The adverb *quite* often precedes the indefinite article *a*.

- The newspaper columnist *caused* quite *a stir* by suggesting that it might be wrong to fund research solely for the purpose of prolonging human life.
- Talking about that sensitive issue will only serve to *stir up a hornet's nest.* Do you really think it's a good idea?

rock the boat　　to cause an unpleasant controversy or debate

- With only two more years to go until retirement, the assistant decided not to *rock the boat* by revealing inaccuracies in the accounting books.
- The discovery of steroid abuse on the college football team has *rocked the boat* for all concerned.

blow the whistle　　to report another's wrongdoing to one's superiors
related form: **whistle-blower** (noun)

- Some companies maintain a free 800 number for callers to *blow the whistle* on wrongdoing.
- The disgruntled employee became a *whistle-blower* when others were paid for unauthorized overtime.

EXERCISES

A.　　**Fill in each blank with the appropriate form of an idiom from this unit.**

1. The citizens' panel has _____ quite _____ _____ by suggesting that the city school system is in need of a major overhaul.

2. The assistant contacted the city attorney's office to _____ _____ _____ on excessive travel expenses by city council members.

3. Reports of widespread cheating among cadets at training facilities has _____ _____ _____ at the highest levels of the Navy.

4. Betty wants to move into her own apartment because her parents are constantly _____ _____ her poor grades and active social life.

5. Why are you _____ such _____ _____ _____ _____ my new hairstyle? Everyone is dyeing their hair different colors now!

6. The police had trouble restraining the crazy man, who was _____ _____ _____ at everyone who passed by.

7. Right after Ms. Johnson _____ _____ _____ her neighbor about the junk in his yard, she realized that a calm approach would have worked better.

8. Polite suggestions aren't making Edward change his bad attitude toward me. One of these days I'll just have to _____ _____ _____ _____ him.

9. Ms. Thompson was passed up unfairly for a promotion for a third time. If I were her, I'd _____ _____ _____ _____ _____!

10. Does it really matter whether it cost $74 or $75 or $76? At this point we're just _____ _____.

B. Choose the statement in the right column that best responds to each question in the left column. Write the appropriate number in the blank.

1. Why do you keep harping on the issue of the housework?

2. Isn't Ann nitpicking to complain about the length of her work breaks?

3. Why were you and your neighbor ranting and raving at each other?

4. What happened to the whistle-blower in your company?

5. What happened when Mark had words with his soccer teammates?

____ a. Because it'll never get done if I don't make a fuss about it.

____ b. I just had it out with him about the noise from his drum set.

____ c. She was fired for rocking the boat.

____ d. He caused quite a stir. I think they'll play better from now on.

____ e. Maybe, but she's had an ax to grind ever since she was refused overtime pay.

C. Use the idioms in your spoken or written answers to the following questions.

1. Do you have any bad or unusual habits that other people in your life *harp on?* What are they?

2. What would you do if you suddenly faced someone who was *ranting and raving?*

3. For what reasons might you *have it out with* a friend or family member? Has this ever happened to you? When?

4. Why do most people hesitate to *rock the boat?* Is this true for you?

5. Can you suggest some good reasons for *blowing the whistle?*

D. Using the idioms from this unit or a previous one, tell a classmate about the last time you had an argument with someone. You may want to include the following:

- who you were arguing with;
- what the argument was about;
- how you expressed yourself;
- what kind of reaction you got;
- whether any points in the argument were unreasonable.

Unit 28
Irritation and Annoyance

eat at to bother, to continue to irritate

GRAMMAR NOTE: This idiom usually occurs in a progressive verb form.

- What's *eating at* you? You're frowning and not responding to me.
- The silly mistakes Joe made on the final exam have been *eating at* him for days.

get on one's nerves to cause irritation or annoyance

USAGE NOTE: The subject is often an annoying sound or repetitive complaint.

- The loud noises coming from the next apartment really *got on Humphrey's nerves.*
- Stop shouting at me like that! It's *getting on my nerves.*

rub the wrong way to irritate and annoy repeatedly

GRAMMAR/USAGE NOTES: An object follows the verb. The subject is usually a person, or the person's words or actions.

- What an unpleasant person your boss is. He *rubbed* me *the wrong way* right from the start.
- Everything he says seems to *rub* me *the wrong way.* It must be the nasal quality of his voice.
- When two people don't hit it off, it's often because they *rub* each other *the wrong way.* (hit it off: see Unit 11)

hit a nerve to be a sensitive point or matter to someone

- When Leroy's friend commented on his still living with his parents, it really *hit a nerve.*
- I could tell by her reaction that I had *hit a nerve* when I mentioned her secrecy about her past.

thorn in the side a lingering situation that continues to annoy someone
related idiom: **fly in the ointment** (a minor drawback or disadvantage)

- The fact that Fred invited his parents to visit us during our first extended vacation in years is still a *thorn in the side.*
- Jed's opposition to our plan is disappointing, but it's really only a *fly in the ointment.*
  (= minor problems)

86

ruffle some feathers   *Large company also 年매* to cause others to be annoyed by one's actions

GRAMMAR NOTE: A possessive noun or possessive adjective can be substituted for *some*.

■ The employee *ruffled some feathers* when he took his complaint to the top levels of management.

■ Samantha succeeded in *ruffling her dad's feathers* by staying out past her midnight curfew.

get into one's hair   to annoy by being too close and in the way

↔ get out of my hair

GRAMMAR/USAGE NOTES: The participial form of this idiom often follows the verb *keep*.

■ The small children kept *getting into the housekeeper's hair,* so she sent them outside to play.

■ Instead of *getting into my hair* all the time, why don't you find a good book to read?

pet peeve   a small thing or action that regularly annoys someone

GRAMMAR/USAGE NOTES: This noun form can be made plural. The annoying thing or action is usually difficult to control.

■ The sound of silverware scraping against a plate is a silly *pet peeve* of mine.

■ People's annoying habits, such as snoring in bed, are common *pet peeves.*

broken record   someone who repeats the same idea or complaint

GRAMMAR NOTE: The subject is always a person, and the verb *be* or *sound like* is usually used.

■ Harriet is a *broken record* when she complains about the air-conditioning every day.

■ You sound like a *broken record.* You keep saying you're going to find a job, but you never do anything about it.

EXERCISES

A.   Fill in each blank with the appropriate form of an idiom from this unit. Some sentences may have more than one correct answer.

1. You constantly complain about the broken toilet but make no effort to fix it. You sound just like a _broken_ _record_ .

2. I wonder what's _eating_ _at_ Mario. He's been acting bothered all day.

3. Jack's refusal to help us move is still a _thorn_ _in_ _the_ _side_ for me.

4. I wish that Kyle would stop shaking her leg nervously like that. It's one of my _pet_ _peeves_ about her.

5. You could tell by Ellen's reaction that you _hit_ ~~the~~ _a_ _nerve_ by mentioning her recent weight gain. She's very sensitive about it.

6. My supervisor was annoyed that I talked to *his* supervisor about the problem, and both of them complained to *their* supervisors. I guess I really _ruffled_ _some_ _feathers_

7. Could you please turn down the music? I'm trying to concentrate and the noise is beginning to _get_ ~~on~~ _my_ ~~nerves~~ _nerves._

8. Larry and Karla don't get along well. It seems that they _rub_ each other _the_ _wrong_ _way_ almost every time they talk.

9. Phillip, could you please keep the children out of the art studio? I'm trying to paint, and they're _getting_ _into_ _my_ _hair_ .

B. Choose the statement in the right column that best responds to each question in the left column. Write the appropriate number in the blank.

1. Doesn't constant interference from the boss's son get on your nerves?

2. Gloria's comments are often such a thorn in the side, aren't they?

3. Pat's been acting annoyed recently. Do you know what's been eating at her?

4. Why has Bob rubbed me the wrong way since I first met him?

5. I know I sound like a broken record, but could you please stop biting your nails?

_2_ a. Yes. She manages to hit a nerve with almost every remark.

_4_ b. Maybe it's because he gets into your hair all the time.

_5_ c. I didn't realize I was doing it. I know it's your pet peeve.

_1_ d. Yes, but I'd ruffle some feathers if I complained.

_3_ e. Although she likes her job, not getting a raise has been a fly in the ointment lately.

C. Use the idioms in your spoken or written answers to the following questions.

1. Did you use to *get into your parent's hair* as a child? What did you do? How about your brothers and/or sisters?

2. Do any of your family members or friends ever sound like a *broken record?* What do they say?

3. What are the potential benefits and risks of *ruffling some feathers* at work in order to accomplish something?

4. How would you know if you *hit a nerve* when speaking with someone?

5. Can you describe the kind of person who *rubs* you *the wrong way?*

D. Using the idioms from this unit or a previous one, tell a classmate about things that irritate or annoy you. You may want to include the following:

- things or actions that regularly annoy you;
- kinds of people who often irritate you;
- what problems bother you for a long time;
- what noises annoy you.

Unit 29
Concern and Regret

weigh on one's mind   to concern greatly, to preoccupy with thought

USAGE NOTE: The adverb *heavily* can be added after the verb *weigh*.

- Her mother's ongoing health problem has been **weighing on Jill's mind** throughout the year.
- Mr. Grave's decision to fire several long-term employees **weighed** heavily **on his mind** for days.

lose sleep over   not to be able to sleep well because of something

USAGE NOTE: Adjectives such as *any, much,* or *a lot of* can be added before the noun *sleep*.

- The problem at school can't be so bad that it's worth **losing sleep over**.
- Mark has **lost** a lot of **sleep over** the robbery in his neighborhood.

raise eyebrows   to attract the concern or disapproval of others
also: **raise an eyebrow**

GRAMMAR/USAGE NOTES: These idioms are used when someone's actions or words cause others to disapprove. The adjective *some* can precede the plural form *eyebrows*.

- The boss's new hairpiece **raised** some **eyebrows** around the office.
- When I told my dad that I was going to stay up late, he looked up from his newspaper and **raised an eyebrow** at me.

make much of   to consider important and worth talking about

USAGE NOTE: The adverb *so* can be added before *much*.

- The small store owners **made much of** the fact that the new shopping mall would seriously affect their business.
- Don't **make** so **much of** the situation. It will probably resolve itself in a few days anyway.

not give a thought (to)   not to worry or think about something, to ignore

GRAMMAR NOTE: A noun or pronoun follows the verb *give* when *to* is not used.

- I'm more than glad to watch your children in an emergency. Do**n't give** it **a thought**.
- Herbert does**n't give a thought to** my schedule when he makes his business trip arrangements.

be too bad   to be regrettable, to be sorry

related idioms: **What a shame, What a pity**

GRAMMAR/USAGE NOTES: The related idioms are used in exclamatory forms. All three idioms are often followed by a noun clause starting with *that*.

- It*'s too bad* that the corner grocery store burned down. Now we have to use the large supermarket, where the produce selection is terrible.

- *What a shame* that Debbie's not able to stay with us this summer. I was looking forward to seeing her.

- Your new pair of pants is ruined because of the grease spot. *What a pity!*

kick oneself for   to regret one's past action or inaction

USAGE NOTE: A gerund (verb + *-ing*) often follows this idiom.

- I could *kick myself for* having made that rude comment in front of all my colleagues.

- You shouldn't *kick yourself for* something that really isn't your responsibility.

come back to haunt   to return as a problem from someone's past

USAGE NOTE: This idiom is used when a past action has a regrettable effect on present circumstances, or when someone predicts that a present action will have a regrettable effect on future circumstances.

- The criminal's past *came back to haunt* him when the police falsely arrested him for armed robbery.

- If you don't take care of the matter now, it will certainly *come back to haunt* you later.

EXERCISES

A.   Fill in each blank with the appropriate form of an idiom from this unit.

JAY: Darn it, Jean, I could _____ _____ _____ having made that
        ₁

appointment with the insurance agent. I don't need to renew my car insurance.

JEAN: What are you saying, Jay? That remark would _____ _____ down at the
         ₂

police station.

JAY: I bet it would, but I meant that I'm selling my car.

JEAN: What? I thought you loved your car.

JAY: I do, but it's old, and the high cost of maintaining it is _____ heavily
        ₃

_____ _____ _____ these days, not to mention on my wallet.

JEAN: That _____ _____ _____. Are you _____ much _____
         ₄   ₅

_____ it?

JAY: Yes, I am, as a matter of fact. I haven't been sleeping well recently, and you

know how I always _____ _____ _____ the importance of getting
                    ₆

enough sleep!

JEAN: I know. You always need eight hours every night no matter what.

JAY: That's right! Anyway, back to the car, I need the cash.

JEAN: What do you need money for?

JAY: I'm going to invest everything in InternetScape, one of the newest on-line service companies on the World Wide Web.

JEAN: Wow, that kind of risky investment in the stock market might _____
7
_____ _____ _____ you later if you're not careful. I'm a little worried for you.

JAY: I would _____ _____ it _____ _____ if I were you. Besides, it's
8
only a couple of thousand dollars.

JEAN: OK. I hope you're right!

B. Choose the statement in the right column that best responds to each question in the left column. Write the appropriate number in the blank.

1. Is James kicking himself for not accepting the promotion and transfer?
2. Did Jane's complaints about work conditions raise any eyebrows?
3. Do you know that I'm still losing sleep over my argument with Bernice?
4. Do you think your sarcastic comment will come back to haunt you later?
5. Why did Chris make so much of the fact that there won't be a school dance?

____ a. What a shame that friends like you are angry at each other.
____ b. He certainly is. The mistake still weighs on his mind.
____ c. I don't know, but it's too bad that it was called off.
____ d. Not really. Her boss is too lazy to even raise an eyebrow!
____ e. Probably, but at the time I didn't give that any thought.

C. Use the idioms in your spoken or written answers to the following questions.

1. Some people *lose sleep over* problems that most people consider trivial or unimportant. Can you think of any examples? Does this ever happen to you? Explain.
2. What kind of comment would you *kick yourself for* having made?
3. What are some actions that might *raise eyebrows?*
4. Does your future *weigh on your mind,* or do you *not give* it *much thought?* Explain.
5. What kind of serious mistake might *come back to haunt you?*

D. Using the idioms from this unit or a previous one, develop a dialogue or role play involving two or three friends who are concerned about a serious matter. You may want to include the following:

- what matter is of concern to them;
- how each friend feels about the matter;
- whether the matter has attracted the attention of others;
- any regrets that the friends have.

Unit 30
Tolerance and Frustration

put up with   to tolerate or accept unwillingly
  also: **grin and bear**
- We moved to a different picnic spot because we couldn't **put up with** the noise of a tractor mower nearby.
- When the government decides to raise income taxes, we generally **grin and bear it.**

be fed up with   to be unable to accept any longer
  also: **be sick (and tired) of**
- I'**m fed up with** my roommate's sloppy habits. If he doesn't make an effort to reform, I'll ask him to move out.
- *Aren't* you *sick and tired of* the rat race of urban life? (**rat race**: see Unit 13)

put an end to   to eliminate, to abolish
  also: **do away with**
- It would be nice to **put an end to** all poverty, but unfortunately that is probably wishful thinking. (**wishful thinking**: see Unit 10)
- Major nations of the world recently voted to **do away with** all short-range nuclear missiles.

the last straw   the final action by another person that cannot be ignored
- When the desk clerk was late to work for the third time, it was **the last straw** for his supervisor.
- What, you took some money from my wallet again without my permission? That's **the last straw!** I'm never lending you any money again, and stay out of my room!

draw the line at   to establish a certain limit at
- The boss can accept some challenges from her employees, but she **draws the line at** insubordination.
- Jerry's parents **drew the line at** five friends for his birthday sleepover party.

at the end of one's rope   feeling frustrated and not knowing what to do
- Caring for her two young children every day had Terry **at the end of her rope,** so she arranged morning day care for them.
- I feel like I'm **at the end of my rope** in this job. Nothing ever seems to go right, and it doesn't satisfy me anymore.

pull one's hair out over to remain upset about a frustrating situation

GRAMMAR/USAGE NOTES: This idiom often occurs as a gerund phrase after the expression *There's no sense. . . .*

- There's no sense *pulling your hair out over* that regrettable incident. What's done is done.
- For quite some time Craig was *pulling his hair out over* the situation, until he realized that thinking about it was a waste of time.

beat one's head against the wall to be completely frustrated in one's efforts

- You're just *beating your head against the wall* if you think that you can really change the political system.
- Each time I complained about the smell from the nearby dump, I felt that I was just *beating my head against the wall.*

EXERCISES

A. **Fill in each blank with the appropriate form of an idiom from this unit. Some sentences may have more than one correct answer.**

1. First John borrowed my favorite jacket, then he didn't return it for three weeks, and now he has lost it. That's really _____ _____ _____!

2. How can you _____ _____ _____ all that noise while you're studying? I can't.

3. I can't stand doing all the housework myself anymore. I'm really _____ _____ _____ _____ _____ _____.

4. Aren't you _____ _____ _____ this terrible morning commute? We should take the bus to work.

5. Kate is never going to change her mind, so you're just _____ _____ _____ _____ _____ _____ if you still try.

6. Linda didn't mind volunteering a couple of hours of her time last week, but this week she _____ _____ _____ _____ four more hours.

7. There's no sense _____ _____ _____ _____ _____ that unfortunate incident. It's water under the bridge.

8. Wouldn't it be nice to _____ _____ _____ _____ all forms of discrimination in the world?

B. **Choose the statement in the right column that best responds to each question in the left column. Write the appropriate number in the blank.**

1. Aren't you sick and tired of the violence in today's world?	____ a. I should. All this volunteering has me at the end of my rope.
2. Isn't Bettina fed up with her coach's constant criticism?	____ b. I can't. This last incident was the last straw.
3. How can you put up with Raymond's constant lying and pettiness?	____ c. I certainly am. I wish we could do away with all weapons.
4. What's the sense in pulling your hair out over Jeff's carefree lifestyle?	____ d. Yes, but if she wants to stay on the team, she has to grin and bear it.
5. Shouldn't you draw the line at four committee meetings in one week?	____ e. You're right. He'll never change, so why beat my head against the wall?

Tolerance and Frustration   Unit 30

C. Use the idioms in your spoken or written answers to the following questions.

1. What are some common problems or irritations in life that you have to *put up with?*

2. Where might you *draw the line at* helping a friend in need?

3. Do you ever feel *fed up with* anything? What do you do to handle your frustrations?

4. Have you ever felt like you were *beating your head against the wall?* What happened?

5. What things or situations in your life would you like to *do away with?*

D. Using the idioms from this unit or a previous one, develop a dialogue or role play involving two or three co-workers who are facing problems at work. You may want to include the following:

- the source of the frustration;
- each co-worker's reaction to the situation;
- any action that is taken.

94

Review: Units 21–30

A. Circle the expression that best completes each sentence.

1. Jessie was all excited about visiting the amusement park, but unfortunately I have to tell her that we can't go. I hate to _____ like that.
   a. get into the spirit
   b. keep a straight face
   c. break her heart

2. You can tell from the high quality of his products that he _____ his work.
   a. takes pride in
   b. has it out with
   c. doesn't give a thought to

3. Could you tell the children to go to their rooms? They're just _____.
   a. stealing the show
   b. getting in our hair
   c. throwing us for a loop

4. The smell from the farm next door is almost intolerable to me. I don't know how you can _____ it.
   a. kick yourself for
   b. harp on
   c. put up with

5. Sally looks like she needs some comfort and advice. Do you think I should offer her _____?
   a. a shoulder to cry on
   b. my pride and joy
   c. the last straw

6. All the players and fans on both sides of the field were _____ as the big championship game started.
   a. taken aback
   b. fired up
   c. stuck up

7. I can tell by the serious look on your face that you _____.
   a. come back to haunt
   b. take a back seat
   c. mean business

8. OK, so Irma lied about the actual cost of the purchase. That doesn't mean that Tony should _____ it.
   a. make a big deal of
   b. have an ax to grind
   c. have words with

9. With opinion polls indicating certain re-election, the president _____ by announcing that he would not run for office again.
   a. dropped a bombshell
   b. went with the crowd
   c. blew his own horn

10. _____ that your brother can't visit us. I was looking forward to seeing him.
    a. What on earth
    b. What a shame
    c. What a hard pill to swallow

B. Indicate whether each statement is TRUE (T) or FALSE (F).

_____ 1. If you have to grin and bear something, it means you're crazy about it.

_____ 2. Someone who has a big head might rub you the wrong way.

_____ 3. You would want to put an end to something that was music to your ears.

_____ 4. If you have hurt someone's feelings unnecessarily, it might weigh on your mind.

_____ 5. Someone who toots his or her own horn might sound like a broken record.

_____ 6. If you didn't give a darn about something, you'd probably make much of it.

_____ 7. You'd raise an eyebrow at something that cracked you up.

_____ 8. Someone who's fed up with wrongdoing at work might become a whistle-blower.

_____ 9. You would probably feel sorry for someone who was put on the spot unfairly.

_____ 10. To get something off your chest, you'd have to be tied up in knots.

C. Complete the puzzle with the missing parts of the idioms in the sentences below.

ACROSS

2. Elijah took _____ on the man begging for money.
3. Let's watch the old movie just for _____ .
6. All you do is rant and _____ when you're upset.
7. What in the _____ was that noise?
10. Greg's marriage proposal took Linda by _____ .
11. You shouldn't let a minor problem _____ at you.
13. Why did you throw a wet _____ on our plans?
15. Keep your _____ up no matter what happens.
16. Fingernail-chewing is a pet _____ of mine.
17. The delay in our trip was a small fly in the _____ .
18. Martin's comment stirred up a hornet's _____ .

DOWN

1. I drew the _____ at ten hours of unpaid overtime.
3. Why are you always so serious? _____ up!
4. Splitting _____ is not going to help us at all.
5. That joke really tickled my funny _____ .
8. The mistake isn't a _____ matter to me.
9. It's late. We _____ as well go to bed.
11. The politician's arrest raised _____ in town.
12. Jack is so busy that he's at the end of his _____ .
13. You'll rock the _____ if you file a complaint.
14. Wendy's baby is the _____ of her eye.

Unit 31
Agreement and Disagreement

see eye to eye   to agree completely
- I'm glad that we *see eye to eye* on all aspects of the multimillion dollar contract. Please sign here.
- My parents and I didn't *see eye to eye* about many aspects of my life, so I moved into a friend's place.

go along (with)   to agree, to conform

USAGE NOTE: The nouns *idea, suggestion,* or *recommendation* often follow the preposition *with.*
- Mrs. Charleston is the one who plans all details of their travels, while Mr. Charleston and the children just *go along.*
- Wouldn't it be easier to *go along with* the committee's recommendation than to fight it at a higher level?

on the same wavelength   to be thinking exactly the same thing, by coincidence or due to experience
- I was about to make the same comment you just made. We must be *on the same wavelength.*
- The mountain rescue team worked efficiently to find the lost hiker because their minds were all operating *on the same wavelength.*

side with   to support or favor another person or persons
- You would *side with* me no matter what happened, wouldn't you? Otherwise, how could you be a true friend?
- Even though I sympathize with your rationale, I'd have to *side with* your opposition on that matter.

You can say that again.   I completely agree with what you said
- SAL: TGIF—Thank goodness it's Friday.
  BEN: *You can say that again.*
- When Matt praised the mild climate that made wearing short pants and short-sleeved shirts possible in the winter, several people responded, *"You can say that again."*

be for   to be in favor of, to support
opposite meaning: **be (dead set) against** (to oppose)

- How can you *be for* that ballot proposal when you know it benefits only a few powerful construction firms?
- Milton will never be convinced that the court decision was correct. He's *been dead set against* a guilty verdict right from the start.

be at odds with   to be in conflict with

- It's not pleasant *being at odds with* you. Couldn't we sit down and solve the problem intelligently?
- The chairperson's advisors *were at odds with* each other over what course of action to take, and they never did take a clear position.

war of words   a continual spoken or written exchange between opposing sides

- Through ten years of writing to the editor's column, the two antagonists pursued their *war of words* on various social and political issues.
- The career diplomat was tired of the *war of words* dominating the lengthy peace talks. Neither side was willing to compromise, and both had threatened to leave.

EXERCISES

A.   **Fill in each blank with the appropriate form of an idiom from this unit.**

1. The committee vote was unanimous because all the members _____ _____ _____ _____ on appropriating the emergency funds.

2. So far we agree on all of the important issues. Unlike other times, we seem to be _____ _____ _____ _____ this time.

3. WIFE: I'm so glad that we're finally on vacation.
   HUSBAND: _____ _____ _____ _____ _____!

4. The Nelsons finally got divorced because they had grown tired of the constant _____ _____ _____ between them.

5. The high school football and soccer coaches _____ _____ _____ _____ each other over how to share the only athletic field on campus.

6. I really don't care what we do this weekend, so you decide and I'll just _____ _____.

7. Who _____ you _____ in this year's mayoral race?

8. When Mr. Jackson was asked to settle a problem between his wife and his daughter, he _____ _____ his daughter.

B. Choose the statement in the right column that best responds to each question in the left column. Write the appropriate number in the blank.

1. Was the boss against Peggy's ideas for the office party again this year?

2. Isn't it unfortunate that we almost never see eye to eye on things these days?

3. What party are you siding with in the race for president?

4. Isn't it nice that we're not at odds with each other so much recently?

5. How much longer are we going to continue this war of words between us?

____ a. As long as it takes for you to see my point and to go along.

____ b. I'd have to say I'm for the Democratic party this time.

____ c. No, this time he went along with her suggestions.

____ d. I know. I guess we're just not on the same wavelength anymore.

____ e. You can say that again.

C. Use the idioms in your spoken or written answers to the following questions.

1. In what ways do you *see eye to eye* with your parents or other family members? In what ways *are* you *at odds with* them?

2. Do you have a friend with whom you are *on the same wavelength* most of the time? Give some examples.

3. When was the last time that you were involved in a *war of words?* What happened?

4. What could someone say that would prompt you to respond, *"You can say that again"*?

5. *Are* you *for* or *against* the death penalty for serious crimes such as murder? Explain your position.

D. Using the idioms from this unit or a previous one, develop a dialogue or role play about two or more people who are having an argument. You may want to include the following:

■ the nature of the conflict between them;

■ who supports or opposes one side or the other, and in what way;

■ the nature of their verbal exchange;

■ whether the people ever manage to agree.

Unit 32
Responsibility

leave to   to give someone responsibility or authority for

GRAMMAR NOTE: An object follows the verb *leave*, often in the form of the pronoun *it*.

- Instead of doing most of the work herself, the single mother should *leave* more of it *to* her two teenage sons.
- *Leave* it *to* Adam to make the graduation party a success! He really is a good organizer.

dump on   to assign work unfairly, to criticize unfairly

GRAMMAR NOTE: An object follows the verb *dump*.

- Why did Dad *dump* this chore *on* me and not you? Oh, yeah, you have a big school project and I don't!
- In most organizations, the work that nobody wants to do gets *dumped on* the newest employees.

take on   to accept as a responsibility or task, to undertake

GRAMMAR NOTE: This idiom is separable and requires an object.

- It's not a good idea to *take on* more than you are capable of doing at one time.
- The retired Navy man was at first hesitant about doing volunteer work, but eventually he was glad that he had *taken* it *on*.

take over   to assume control of

GRAMMAR NOTE: This idiom is separable.

- When Mrs. Custer died, her son Randolph *took over* the family business, and now it's thriving.
- When the city manager's position became available, a more experienced administrator *took* it *over* and made a number of changes.

look after   to watch, to supervise
also: **keep an eye on**

- Would you mind *looking after* the guests by yourself for a while? I have to make an important phone call.
- The baby-sitter forgot to *keep an eye on* the smallest child, who wandered into the garage and began playing with a sharp tool.

see about   to be responsible for doing
 also: **see to**
 USAGE NOTE: These idioms are often followed by a gerund (verb + -*ing*).

■ There's a leak in the drain, and I've got to rush off to work now. Could you *see about* getting the plumbing fixed?

■ In our family, each member *sees to* his or her own clothing, snacks, dishes, and so on.

see through   to complete a responsibility to the end
 also: **carry through**
 GRAMMAR NOTE: These idioms are separable.

■ Why don't you *see through* your craft projects instead of just letting them lie around the garage?

■ The fund-raiser was a huge success, mainly because Inge was recruited to *carry* it *through.*

carry the ball   to have the main responsibility for completing an assignment
 opposite meaning: **drop the ball**

■ When the parent association president suddenly quit, Annette agreed to *carry the ball* by becoming the temporary president.

■ I wish that Sam hadn't *dropped the ball* on the Havers deal. Then there wouldn't be this complication.

carry one's weight   to do one's share in completing responsibilities

■ The emergency crews cleaned up the industrial accident in less than two hours because they all *carried their weight.*

■ The other employees don't like Melody because she doesn't *carry her weight* around the office.

EXERCISES

A.   Fill in each blank with the appropriate form of an idiom from this unit. Some sentences may have more than one correct answer.

I.   Mrs. Olsen's teenage daughter Melinda didn't want to _____ _____

her two-year-old sister for an hour. Mrs. Olsen got angry and complained that

Melinda didn't _____ _____ _____ around the house. Mrs. Olsen had
                              2

to _____ _____ opening a new account at the bank, and had no choice
        3

but to _____ it _____ Melinda to baby-sit.
              4

II.   Sam Ford was upset. His boss had just _____ an urgent assignment
                                                        5

_____ him before a three-day holiday weekend. At first Sam refused to

_____ _____ the extra work, but his boss made it clear that he was the
        6

one who was expected to _____ _____ _____ on this matter. Sam
                                      7

didn't want to _____ _____ someone's work in the middle, but he figured
                      8

that he had no choice but to _____ it _____.
                                      9

B. Choose the statement in the right column that best responds to each question in the left column. Write the appropriate number in the blank.

1. Would you mind looking after the children for a while?

_____ a. He can't see to the heavy chores since his back operation.

2. Why does Dad always dump the hardest yard work on me?

_____ b. I understand that Eduardo has been assigned to carry the ball.

3. Who was chosen to see the computer project through?

_____ c. Because he doesn't carry his weight like the rest of the workers.

4. Why is it necessary to keep an eye on the newest employee?

_____ d. Not at all. You can leave it to me to watch them.

5. Did Karen take on additional duties when Larry quit?

_____ e. Yes, she took over all of his business accounts.

C. Use the idioms in your spoken or written answers to the following questions.

1. If someone asked you to *keep an eye on* things while he or she was away on vacation, what would you be expected to do?

2. When was the last time that something was *dumped on* you? How did you feel?

3. What do you have to *see about* doing today? What do you have to *see to* in the near future?

4. What things in your home can you repair yourself and what do you *leave to* a repair technician?

5. Are you the kind of person who often *carries the ball* in your activities? Explain.

D. Using the idioms from this unit or a previous one, tell a classmate about how work is shared in your family. You may want to include the following:

- what each family member is responsible for;
- whether everyone shares equally in the work;
- who needs to be supervised more than others;
- whether work is ever unfairly assigned.

Unit 33
Support and Proof

back up (on)   to support, to corroborate
related form: **backup** (reinforcement)
GRAMMAR NOTE: *Back up* is separable.

- I didn't leave the office door unlocked overnight. You've got to *back* me *up on* that, or I'm in big trouble with the boss.
- The police officer called for a *backup* before he followed the suspect into the building.

stand up for   to defend, to argue on behalf of
also: **go to bat for**

- One of the strengths of democracy is that every citizen can *stand up for* his or her rights in a court of law.
- It was great for you to *go to bat for* me when someone questioned my dedication to the company.

come out for   to voice one's opinion in favor of something, to endorse
USAGE NOTE: This idiom is used for political endorsements and more formal kinds of support of others.

- The Republican party boss *came out for* the young newcomer instead of the incumbent in the congressional election.
- The mayor *came out for* the proposed budget, but the city council wouldn't even consider it.

stand behind   to firmly believe in and support
USAGE NOTE: This idiom is followed by an object. It is used when integrity or truth is in question, and can be modified by *100 percent*.

- No matter what the lie detector test supposedly reveals, I *stand behind* my statement 100 percent.
- When her son was accused of stealing some merchandise, Mrs. Edison *stood behind* him and never doubted his innocence.

pull for   to show one's support for, to encourage
USAGE NOTE: This idiom is usually used in a progressive verb form.

- Sue has been in the hospital for five weeks since the accident, and we've been *pulling for* her the whole time.
- Good luck in all of your track events. We'll be up in the stands with the rest of the fans *pulling for* you.

jump on the bandwagon   to join in doing something that many other people are doing

- When a popular idea starts to spread, people are quick to *jump on the bandwagon.*
- At first a few community members were opposed to the park proposal, but after further discussions they *jumped on the bandwagon.*

not have a leg to stand on   to have no justification

- I don't see how you can argue that way. You do*n't have a leg to stand on.*
- The defense lawyer tried to give the criminal fair representation, but it was obvious to all that he did*n't have a leg to stand on.*

paper trail   materials that establish a chronology of past events

- The clerk couldn't find any record of the transaction, but she promised to check the *paper trail* through the cashier's office and the customer service desk.
- For tax purposes it's best to leave a *paper trail* for all business deductions in case there's an audit, and you have to provide proof of the expenses.

acid test   the ultimate test or proof

- Our new four-by-four truck has been able to handle all the hills so far, but this steep one will be the *acid test!*
- The *acid test* of any movie is whether the public is willing to pay to see it.

bear out   to eventually show to be true

GRAMMAR NOTE: This idiom is separable.

- My advice may seem strange to you now, but time will *bear* me *out.*
- All the evidence in the case *bore out* the truth of her statements.

EXERCISES

A.   Fill in each blank with the appropriate form of an idiom from this unit.

1. In searching the defendant's business files, the detectives were able to establish a _____ _____ tying the defendant to the crime.

2. When Sally saw that all of her friends were connected to the Internet, she thought it was time to _____ _____ _____ _____ too.

3. The makers of the new rocket were confident of its design, but they were well aware that the _____ _____ would be when it was launched into orbit for the first time.

4. The politician stated publicly that she _____ 100 percent _____ her assistant, who was charged with influence peddling.

5. I'm sure that you'll win the case in small claims court. Your opponent does _____ _____ _____ _____ _____ _____ _____.

6. During the final match of the tennis tournament, the crowd _____ _____ the unranked player, who was giving the top-ranked player a real challenge.

7. Right now you don't want to accept the wisdom of my advice, but time will _____ me _____.

8. If the police question your whereabouts on the night of the murder, I can _____ _____ your alibi.

9. After carefully studying the information presented to them, members of the citizens' committee _____ _____ _____ stricter controls on gun ownership.

10. None of Ben's friends _____ _____ _____ him when the teacher falsely accused him of cheating on a test.

B. Choose the statement in the right column that best responds to each question in the left column. Write the appropriate number in the blank.

1. Can you or can't you stand behind me on the legal matter?

2. Is Mayor Wilson coming out for the innovative crime prevention plan?

3. Have you been able to track the paper trail on my credit card charge yet?

4. Are you still pulling for your wife to win the triathlon?

5. Would you stand up for your brother if he were confronted by the school bully?

____ a. I told you I can't. I don't think you have a leg to stand on.

____ b. Not yet, but our investigation should bear out your claim.

____ c. He just announced that he's jumping on the bandwagon.

____ d. I would, but I don't think that he needs any backup!

____ e. Naturally I am, but this is the acid test of her endurance.

C. Use the idioms from this unit in your spoken or written answers to the following questions.

1. What do you think would be the *acid test* of a politician's ability?

2. If you were a police officer, in what situations would you call for a *backup?*

3. If there were a political movement to classify tobacco as an addictive drug and to outlaw its use, would you *jump on the bandwagon?* Why or why not?

4. Is there anything that cannot presently be proven true but you think that time will *bear out?* What?

5. Do you *stand behind* the policies of your government? Why or why not?

D. Using the idioms from this unit or a previous one, develop a dialogue or role play in which two or more people are discussing legislation to control the registration and ownership of guns. You may want to include the following:

■ who has joined in supporting the legislation, and why they firmly believe in it;

■ who cannot endorse the legislation, and why they feel there's no justification for it;

■ whether other people have voiced their opinion in favor of it;

■ what the ultimate test of such legislation would be.

Unit 34
Assistance and Advice

lend a (helping) hand   to offer assistance, to help
also: **help out**

GRAMMAR NOTE: Both idioms can be used with or without an object.

- It was very kind of you to **lend a helping hand** with my groceries, young man. Perhaps I can **lend** you **a hand** some day.
- OK, so you're too busy to **help** me **out** with balancing the checkbook now. Can you **help out** later?

pitch in   to do one's share to help

USAGE NOTE: This idiom can be used when people contribute time or money to a good cause.

- Cleaning the house is a much easier task when all members of the family **pitch in.**
- Most of the neighborhood **pitched in** to rebuild the playground equipment after it had been vandalized.

take under one's wing   to adopt as one of the family; to supervise someone's training

GRAMMAR/USAGE NOTES: An object follows the verb *take*. The object is usually a person or animal who is cared for or taught by others.

- The Bigelows had an extra room in their house, so they **took** a homeless mother and child **under their wing.**
- The retired musician **took** the young boy **under her wing** and taught him to play the piano.
- A kind old man **took** the lost puppy **under his wing** until the owner could be found.

words of wisdom   important ideas to consider

USAGE NOTE: The verb *offer* is often used.

- As you get older, you'll appreciate your grandfather's **words of wisdom** more.
- The high school principal offered the graduating class some **words of wisdom** about social and moral responsibilities.

speak to   to consult

USAGE NOTE: This idiom is used to request a consultation with someone in authority or with knowledge.

- Excuse me, who could I **speak to** about returning this merchandise?
- Would you like to **speak to** one of our financial advisors?

turn to   to seek help or advice from
also: **look to**

- Whenever Ms. Turner's car breaks down on the highway, she *turns to* her auto insurance company representative for assistance.
- Don't *look to* me for advice on selecting a new stereo system. I don't know a tweeter from a woofer.

steer straight   to provide with sensible advice for making the right choices in life

GRAMMAR NOTE: An object follows the verb in active form.

- The teenager was headed for a life of crime, but a caring counselor *steered* her *straight,* and now she's an honor student.
- How can children be *steered straight* in life if both parents work and time together is spent mainly in front of the TV?

sound out   to sense how someone thinks or feels

GRAMMAR/USAGE NOTES: This idiom is separable. It is often used when someone tries to uncover another person's thoughts or feelings, sometimes indirectly.

- The post office worker *sounded out* her colleagues about her suggestions for improving letter and package handling.
- I don't know if he would support our proposal or not. Why don't you *sound* him *out* about it without actually telling him the details?

bum steer   bad advice, poor recommendation

USAGE NOTE: This idiom is often used with the verb *give* and in exclamations.

- We were hoping for a good meal at the restaurant that Stacey recommended, but I'm sorry to say that she gave us a *bum steer.*
- That old, dirty ghost town that the guidebook recommended wasn't worth driving 150 miles to see. What a *bum steer!*

EXERCISES

A. Fill in each blank with the appropriate form of an idiom from this unit. Some sentences may have more than one correct answer.

1. Could I please _____ _____ the manager about a salesclerk who treated me quite rudely?

2. The audience was listening intently to the _____ _____ _____ being offered by the renowned family therapist.

3. The artist was struck by the young boy's detailed drawings, so she _____ him _____ _____ _____ and became his personal instructor.

4. Everyone else has put in a couple of hours helping on the project. Can't you find some time to _____ _____ too?

5. If you ever have a problem and need someone to _____ _____, you can always depend on me for advice.

6. What a _____ _____ Ted gave us by recommending that lousy repair shop!

7. Isn't it worth trying to _____ the young criminal _____ one more time? She may listen to our advice this time.

(continued on next page)

8. Try to be subtle when you _____ Wallie _____ on his feelings about our throwing a farewell party for him.

9. This box is too heavy for me to carry alone. Would you mind _____ _____ _____ _____?

B. Choose the statement in the right column that best responds to each question in the left column. Write the appropriate number in the blank.

1. Who gave you a bum steer on that financial investment?

2. Could you help me out with preparations for the picnic?

3. When I move overseas, would you mind taking my pet dog under your wing?

4. Was Alice satisfied with the psychiatrist she turned to?

5. Was Carl able to lend a hand to the young man in trouble with the law?

____ a. I don't know. I'll have to sound out my wife on adopting an animal.

____ b. It was the salesperson I spoke to at the brokerage firm.

____ c. Sure. I'd be more than glad to pitch in with arrangements.

____ d. He tried to steer him straight, but to no avail.

____ e. Yes, she claims to have benefited from his words of wisdom.

C. Use the idioms in your spoken or written answers to the following questions.

1. Who do you **turn to** when you need advice? Who looks to you?

2. Tell about the last time that you **pitched in** to help a friend. How did you become involved? What happened?

3. What animal might you **take under your wing** if you found it injured?

4. Have you ever **lent a helping hand** to a stranger? What did you do?

5. What **words of wisdom** have your parents offered that you have found to be true? Have they ever given you a **bum steer?**

D. Using the idioms from this unit or a previous one, develop a presentation about a time when you needed to ask someone for advice. You can create an imaginary situation. You may want to include the following:

- the matter you needed advice on;
- the person you asked advice from;
- the person's willingness to advise you;
- what ideas the person offered you;
- the effect the advice had on you;
- your final opinion of the advice the person gave you.

Unit 35
Effort and Perseverance

get after   to remind about doing something, to urge to do
related idiom: **keep after** (to remind constantly)

- If you want the project to be done, you'll have to *get after* Todd right away and *keep after* him until he buys the necessary materials.
- The Motor Vehicles Department had to *get after* the used-car dealership to register some unlicensed vehicles on the lot.

step up   to increase, to intensify
related idiom: **turn it up a notch** (to adjust upwardly in strength or effort)
GRAMMAR/USAGE NOTES: *Step up* is separable, and *effort* is often used as the object.

- The Coast Guard *stepped up* its efforts to find the sailors missing at sea for two days.
- We'll never win the game if you guys act so sluggish. Come on, it's time to *turn it up a notch!*

give it one's best shot   to try one's best, to put all effort into

- I've never played golf, but I'll *give it my best shot* if you want me to play with you.
- Yousef never dreamed he would win a medal in the martial arts tournament. His plan had always been just to *give it his best shot.*

go overboard   to do too much, to be excessive in one's efforts
USAGE NOTE: The adverb *way*, meaning *far* or *very*, can follow the verb.

- You shouldn't have made so many delicious dishes for our Thanksgiving dinner. You really *went overboard!*
- When Kathy wrote a fifty-page report for a simple weekend assignment, she *went* way *overboard.*

come on strong   to make great effort at the end

- Terry was only in the middle of the group of runners for most of the race, but then she *came on strong* at the end and took first place.
- Our team was losing by three points, but in the fourth quarter they *came on strong* and won the game.

(on) one's second wind   suddenly having more energy to do something
USAGE NOTE: This idiom is usually preceded by *be on* or *get*.

- Candice was feeling tired until 3:00 P.M., when suddenly she felt fine, like she was *on her second wind.*
- Raymond felt sluggish during the first half of the championship match, but then he got *his second wind* and scored the winning goal.

follow up on   to continue one's involvement in, to complete a responsibility
related form: **follow-up** (noun)

- Detective Kepper was assigned to *follow up on* the case of an actor who mysteriously disappeared during a film shoot.
- Thanks for calling me and checking on the carpet installation. Everything's fine, and I appreciate your *follow-up* on the sale.

EXERCISES

A.   **Fill in each blank with the appropriate form of an idiom from this unit. Some sentences may have more than one correct answer.**

I.   "One more mile to go," Oliver thought to himself. Having overcome fatigue, he was _____ _____ _____ _____, pulling away from the other runners in the marathon. Or so he thought. He glanced back and saw two other runners who were suddenly _____ _____ _____ in an effort to pass him. Without delay he _____ _____ his own effort and managed a satisfying first-place finish.

II.   Even though my daughter is graduating from high school with honors soon, she hasn't started applying to any universities. I don't really want to _____ _____ her about it because I believe that it's her responsibility to _____ _____ _____ the plans she has made for her future. However, I'm concerned that she isn't _____ _____ _____ _____ _____, and thus could fail to be admitted to a prestigious institution. I don't see any need to _____ _____ and apply to too many places, but with today's competition, I believe it's important to pursue whatever advantage one can.

B. Choose the statement in the right column that best responds to each question in the left column. Write the appropriate number in the blank.

1. We're falling behind the other hikers. Can you turn it up a notch?

2. Would you like me to get after my assistant to correct the error for you?

3. Has Jean stepped up the pace in the bicycle race?

4. Does your son give it his best shot when it comes to helping around the house?

5. Isn't Tony going overboard by sending all his clients a holiday card?

____ a. Yes, and I certainly appreciate your follow-up on the matter.

____ b. Yes, it's close to the end, and she's coming on strong.

____ c. He just wants to follow up on his business contacts so that his customers return.

____ d. I think so. I'm getting my second wind now.

____ e. Only if I constantly keep after him about it.

C. Use the idioms in your spoken or written answers to the following questions.

1. Are you good about *following up on* your responsibilities, or does someone often have to *keep after* you? Explain.

2. When do you have to *step up* your efforts in school? How often does this happen?

3. Have you ever experienced getting *your second wind* before? What were you doing? How did you feel?

4. Would you be willing to *give it your best shot* if you were asked to do an activity that you weren't very good at? Why or why not?

5. Have you ever *gone overboard* to please or satisfy someone? What did you do?

D. Using the idioms from this unit or a previous one, develop a dialogue or role play between two Olympic athletes who have just finished competing against each other. You may want to include the following:

- the event they put effort into;
- any additional energy either one had during the event;
- the effort made at the end;
- the role of their coaches in training them;
- the need to increase the intensity of the training program.

Unit 36
Progress

under way   in progress, having started; in motion, moving

GRAMMAR/USAGE NOTES: This idiom may be joined together into one word. The adverb form of this idiom often follows the verb *get*.

- I'm sorry, but you can't enter the council chambers. The hearing is already ***under way.***
- After three hours of waiting for passengers to board and freight to be loaded, the ship finally got ***underway.***

come along   to be progressing

also: **go along**

GRAMMAR NOTE: These idioms are usually used in a progressive form.

- SHOPPER: How is construction on the shopping mall ***coming along?***

  FOREMAN: It's ***going along*** well, I'm glad to say.

take shape   to develop, to form

USAGE NOTE: This idiom is used in the initial stages of planning something.

- Before the screenwriter puts anything down on paper, the scenes and characters gradually ***take shape*** in her mind.
- The plans for the multinational center are ***taking shape*** nicely. All countries are cooperating on the joint venture.

make headway   to progress or accomplish steadily

USAGE NOTE: Adjectives such as *slow* or *good* can be used to modify the noun *headway*.

- The young basketball player received physical therapy for her knee injury every day but ***made*** only slow ***headway.***
- I'm glad to say I'm ***making*** good ***headway*** in my medical studies. I'll be entering an internship program within three months.

keep up (with)   to maintain the same rate (as), to remain equal (to)

- No matter how long Ronnie spends studying chemistry, it's still hard for him to ***keep up with*** the coursework.
- I walk very quickly for my morning exercise. You can come if you think that you can ***keep up!***

112

catch up (with)   to reach the same level or position as
related idiom: **gain ground (on)** (to advance closer)

■ Bart was absent from school for several weeks, making it impossible for him
to *catch up.*

■ The lead group on the expedition was about a mile ahead of us, but our guide
said that we were *gaining ground.*

So far, so good.   Everything is proceeding well./There haven't been any problems yet.

■ When I asked how the training program was going, Lucy responded, *"So far, so good."*

■ EMPLOYEE: Have you found any errors in the final draft of the document?

   BOSS: No. *So far, so good.*

on a roll   doing well, having a good time

■ The novelist was having the easiest time ever with his fourth book. Every day he sat
down at the computer and was quickly *on a roll.*

■ There's been a tremendous amount of good luck in my life recently. You might say
that I've been *on a roll.*

gain steam   to gain momentum

USAGE NOTE: This idiom is often used for increasingly popular movements or causes.

■ Popular sentiment in favor of pollution cleanup has *gained steam* in recent weeks due
to the terrible accident at Two-Kilometer Bay.

■ The move to recall the lieutenant governor of the state *gained steam* when new
allegations of misconduct were made.

fall behind   not to maintain the same level or position as others

USAGE NOTE: The verbs *be* and *get* can be substituted for *fall.*

■ Doesn't it feel bad to *fall behind* in one's work and then have to struggle to catch up?

■ Whenever I *get behind* in writing to family and friends, I take a pad of paper and pen
and head down to my favorite spot along the lake.

EXERCISES

A.   Fill in each blank with the appropriate form of an idiom from this unit. Some sentences
may have more than one correct answer.

1. At first, progress on the project was slow, but eventually the team _____ good
_____ and completed it on time.

2. Could we slow the pace down a little bit? It's difficult for me to _____
_____ when you're jogging so fast.

3. Mildred is really _____ _____ _____ in her new real estate job. She has
sold three million-dollar properties in the last two weeks.

4. Minu is so lazy that he has _____ _____ in his studies again this semester.

5. Minu is disgusted with his laziness and has vowed to _____ _____
_____ the rest of his class within the next two weeks.

6. Public interest in the concept of a single flat income tax _____ _____ when
several candidates endorsed the concept.

7. Could you please hold your voices down in the hallway? There's a meeting
_____ _____ in this room, and the noise is interfering.

(continued on next page)

8. One way that ideas _____ _____ before work actually begins is through brainstorming with others.

9. Ann: I haven't seen you in a long time, Abe. How's work on your novel _____ _____?

10. Abe: _____ _____, _____ _____!

B. Choose the statement in the right column that best responds to each question in the left column. Write the appropriate number in the blank.

1. How are plans for the proposed regional park taking shape?

2. How is Fay coming along in her graduate studies this year?

3. Is Stan making headway on the short story for the fiction contest?

4. Is the parade down Main Street under way yet?

5. Are our team's speed skaters gaining ground on the leaders in the race?

____ a. Fortunately, she's been able to keep up this semester.

____ b. Yes, he's on a roll, and it's almost finished.

____ c. Community interest in the project is gaining steam.

____ d. Yes, but one of the marching bands has fallen behind.

____ e. They're getting closer and closer. So far, so good.

C. Use the idioms in your spoken or written answers to the following questions.

1. At what time do you generally get *underway* in the morning?

2. Are you *making* good *headway* in your efforts to learn English?

3. Is there any part of your life where you're *falling behind?* What can you do about it?

4. Was there ever a time when you had trouble *keeping up with* others? What were you doing?

5. What plans do you have for the future? How are they *taking shape?*

D. Using the idioms from this unit or a previous one, develop a presentation in which you pretend to be a TV sports commentator reporting on an international track event. You may want to include the following:

- when the event started;
- how the event is progressing;
- which runners can't maintain pace with the leaders;
- if any runner is advancing or taking the lead.

Unit 37
Encouraging and Convincing

Hang in there.   Keep trying./Don't give up.

GRAMMAR/USAGE NOTES: This expression is used as a direct or indirect command when someone needs encouragement in the face of a difficult or unpleasant situation.

- The counselor urged the troubled teenager to *hang in there* and resolve his differences with his parents rather than run away from home.
- We've almost finished drilling out the tooth cavity for the second filling. *Hang in there!*

shot in the arm   a needed boost of energy or encouragement

- The Federal Reserve gave the economy a needed *shot in the arm* when it lowered interest rates by a full percentage point.
- Her words of encouragement were the *shot in the arm* that I needed to complete the last two chapters of my thesis.

pep talk   an encouraging talk or lecture

USAGE NOTE: Although this idiom is often used for sports, it can be applied to other situations as well.

- The volleyball coach gave her team a *pep talk* before the game.
- After a *pep talk* from the sales manager, the sales force doubled its efforts to meet the monthly sales quota.

cheer on   to encourage to do well

GRAMMAR/USAGE NOTES: This idiom is separable and applies mainly to sports.

- Aren't you going to the most important basketball game of the year to *cheer on* our team?
- As the five- and six-year-olds chased the ball around the soccer field, their parents wildly *cheered* them *on.*

talk up   to generate enthusiasm or interest in, to advertise

GRAMMAR/USAGE NOTES: This idiom is separable and is used when an event or item is not well known and people need to be encouraged to participate or have an interest.

- The county fair was the first place that the inventor was able to *talk up* interest in his new kitchen gadget.
- It would be nice if a lot of people came to the first meeting of the neighborhood crime watch committee. Don't forget to *talk* it *up* with your neighbors.

talk into   to convince someone to do something
   opposite meaning: **talk out of**
   GRAMMAR NOTES: The person who is convinced is the object that follows the verb. The prepositions *into* and *of* are often followed by a gerund (verb + *-ing*).

■ Sally was able to **talk** the police officer **into** warning her instead of issuing a citation for jaywalking.

■ Sami was determined to quit school and return home to be with his sick mother, but she **talked** him **out of** it.

bring around to   to change someone's way of thinking, to finally convince
   related idiom: **come around to** (to realize the truth or value of someone's way of thinking)

■ With careful reasoning and desperate pleading, I **brought** him **around to** my point of view regarding the remodeling.

■ If you ever **come around to** our way of thinking, we'd be glad to provide more information on our political action group.

give in to   to relent or acquiesce to someone's demands
   USAGE NOTE: This idiom can also be used for bad habits.

■ Why did you **give in to** Tom so quickly? There's no reason why you should lend him your car.

■ Once Margaret quit smoking cigarettes, she never **gave in to** the urge again.

EXERCISES

A.   **Fill in each blank with the appropriate form of an idiom from this unit.**

I.   Behind by seven points at half-time, the players in the locker room didn't look very confident. The coach thought they needed a _____ _____ _____ _____ , so he gathered them together and gave a spirited _____ _____ . He _____ _____ the positive aspects of their game. He told them that the game wasn't over and that they should _____ _____ _____ . The players became excited, and as they ran onto the field shouting and waving their arms, the fans _____ them _____ .

II.

ALI: Mary, why can't I _____ you _____ _____ my way of thinking? My plan is foolproof.

MARY: Ali, you'll never _____ me _____ your crazy scheme.

ALI: But just listen to my idea once more.

MARY: Forget it, Ali. I'll never _____ _____ _____ you!

B. Choose the statement in the right column that best responds to each question in the left column. Write the appropriate number in the blank.

1. Did you give in to having a cigarette at the party?
2. How did you and Linda bring the others around to your point of view?
3. Wasn't it fun cheering our team on when they came from behind and won?
4. What did the coach tell her players during the half-time pep talk?
5. Was Brian able to talk his parents into buying him a car?

_____ a. We simply talked it up until they were convinced.

_____ b. She told them to hang in there and to do their best.

_____ c. It sure was. And our shouting gave them the shot in the arm that they needed.

_____ d. No, I talked myself out of trying even one again.

_____ e. No, they never came around to his way of thinking.

C. Use the idioms in your spoken or written answers to the following questions.

1. Have you ever been **talked into** doing something that you really didn't want to do? What was it?
2. What kind of **pep talk** could an English teacher give a student who was discouraged about his or her progress in learning the language?
3. Would you **give in to** someone who wanted you to go whitewater rafting? Why or why not?
4. Would you try to **talk** someone **out of** dyeing their hair blue? Why or why not?
5. Do you prefer to be directly involved in playing a sport, or do you prefer to **cheer** the players **on** from the sidelines? Why?

D. Using the idioms from this unit or a previous one, tell a classmate about a real or imagined friend who once needed your encouragement. You may want to include the following:

- why this friend needed encouragement;
- how you encouraged him or her;
- if the friend needed to be convinced of something as well;
- what happened as you tried to convince him or her.

Unit 38
Determination and Stubbornness

bent on   determined, certain in one's actions

USAGE NOTE: This idiom is often preceded by the verb *be* or *seem*.

- Vera is ***bent on*** working out at the gym every day. She says that she loves it and has never felt better.
- No matter what advice I offer to the contrary, Quincy seems ***bent on*** handling the matter through court action.

take a stand   to defend and assert one's point of view

USAGE NOTE: This idiom is often followed by a prepositional phrase with *against*.

- The girls kept teasing their little brother, until finally he got angry and ***took a stand.***
- The senior citizens ***took a stand*** against the removal of the recreation center by organizing a letter-writing campaign to the mayor.

stand one's ground   to hold one's position with determination
also: **stick to one's guns**

USAGE NOTE: *Stand one's ground* is used when others are applying pressure on someone.

- The youngest lawyer on the defense team was able to ***stand her ground*** in court against the prosecution.
- I admire your determination to start your own business. Even though you know that most fail in the first year of operation, you're still ***sticking to your guns!***

go to great lengths   to make a determined effort
also: **go to any length**

GRAMMAR/USAGE NOTES: These idioms are close in meaning to *bend over backwards* (Unit 9). They are usually followed by an infinitive phrase.

- Ruby didn't want to talk to Harvey, so she ***went to great lengths*** to avoid him everywhere in the office.
- Agoraphobia, the fear of open spaces, is a mental illness that has left me stuck at home for days on end. I'd ***go to any length*** to lead a normal life again.

set one's sights on   to be determined to have or to do
also: **have one's sights set on, have one's heart set on**

- There's a beautiful sports car on the dealer's lot that I've already ***set my sights on.***
- A bronze or silver medal wasn't enough for Katrin. She ***had her sights set on*** the gold.
- I ***have my heart set on*** going to school in Chicago.

get one's way   to have matters develop as one wishes
also: **have one's way**

USAGE NOTE: These idioms apply when one consequence is that someone else's wish is not met.

- The two sisters were arguing about who would take a shower first, and the older one *got her way.*
- Why do you always *have your way* in these disagreements? Sometimes *I* should *get my way* too!

put one's foot down   to be determined to control or stop a problem

GRAMMAR NOTE: Even though the possessive adjective *one's* can be made plural, the noun *foot* cannot.

- When the teacher *puts her foot down,* all the children know that she is serious. There are no more problems after that.
- Staying out late was one thing, but Kurt's parents *put their foot down* when he asked to stay out until 2:00 A.M.

stubborn as a mule   very stubborn
also: **pig-headed**

USAGE NOTES: Both idioms can be used with the verb *act*. *Pig-headed* is spelled as one word in some dictionaries and can precede a noun.

- You should learn to be more flexible in your attitude and actions. Sometimes you act *stubborn as a mule,* and I don't like it!
- The *pig-headed* custodian insisted on trying to force the window closed, and naturally the glass broke.

EXERCISES

A.   Fill in each blank with the appropriate form of an idiom from this unit. Some sentences may have more than one correct answer.

1. No one ever seems to challenge Sheila's decision-making authority. Why is it that she always _____ _____ _____?

2. You cannot remain neutral on this issue. Please _____ _____ _____ and support one side or another!

3. Pete's friends tried to pressure him into stealing the car with them even after he told them no, but he _____ _____ _____ and refused to have any part in it.

4. Julie, this mess in your room can't continue. It's time I _____ _____ _____ _____ and insist that you clean it up immediately!

5. Why do you act _____ _____ _____ _____? Once in a while you could try to be flexible, couldn't you?

6. The little girl had already _____ _____ _____ _____ a shiny new wagon in the window of the toy store.

7. Daniel _____ _____ _____ _____ to impress his girlfriend's parents when he met them for the first time.

8. It's really sad that Mr. Larsen seems _____ _____ destroying his health by not eating right, but that's not so uncommon these days.

B. Choose the statement in the right column that best responds to each question in the left column. Write the appropriate number in the blank.

1. Did you take a stand against your manager's misuse of his power?

2. Does your husband still have his sights set on a luxury sedan?

3. Why is Alan bent on ignoring our advice about his quitting school?

4. What makes Sarah so pig-headed when I'm around?

5. Why do you always get your way about sitting in the front seat?

____ a. Yes, but I'm going to stick to my guns and insist on a truck.

____ b. When he's made a decision, he can be stubborn as a mule.

____ c. Yes, we finally put our foot down and told him to stop.

____ d. Because I'll go to any length to avoid sitting in the back!

____ e. She's used to having her way and, unfortunately, so are you!

C. Use the idioms in your spoken or written answers to the following questions.

1. What would you *go to great lengths* to have? To be? To do?

2. Give an example of a time when you were *stubborn as a mule.*

3. Have you ever had to *put your foot down* with a friend? What happened?

4. Is there anything you are *bent on* achieving in life? What is it?

5. Do you think that it is important to *take a stand* against racial discrimination in the world? Share your views.

D. Using the idioms from this unit or a previous one, develop a dialogue or role play involving a parent and a child who can't agree on some matter. You may want to include the following:

- what the child is determined about;
- the parent's reason for objecting;
- whether either is stubborn;
- if both hold their positions, or if they manage to compromise.

Unit 39
Gratitude and Praise

thanks to   because of the generosity of, due to

USAGE NOTE: The person, thing, or situation that is the reason for someone's gratitude follows this idiom.

- *Thanks to* Mr. and Mrs. Jackson, we now have a modern, accurate pitching machine for the ballpark. We are forever grateful for their donation.
- Janelle Woodson will never have to work again, *thanks to* winning the state lottery.

owe it to   to be in someone's debt, to be beholden to

USAGE NOTE: Adverbs such as *a lot* can be substituted for *it*.

- You *owe it to* Maxine for having found such a good contractor to handle your living room extension.
- I *owe a lot to* my close friends for all the support they've given me over the years.

thank one's lucky stars   to be grateful for good fortune

also: **count one's lucky stars**

- We can *thank our lucky stars* that we canceled our plans to take that passenger train that derailed last night.
- Instead of worrying about what you don't have, you should be *counting your lucky stars* for what you do have.

owe someone (one)   to be indebted to someone, to be obliged to return a favor

USAGE NOTE: An adverb such as the idiomatic expression *big time* can be used to intensify the feeling of gratitude.

- Thanks for getting up in the middle of the night and rescuing me from my broken-down car. I *owe you one.*
- I *owe Brittany* big time for finding me a job so soon after I lost my old one.

hand it to   to praise someone for a special accomplishment

GRAMMAR/USAGE NOTES: *It* cannot be changed. The auxiliary *have got to* is often used.

- I've got to *hand it to* Frieda. She had a lot of nerve organizing that anticorruption campaign in her district.
- You've got to *hand it to* anyone who perseveres in the face of adversity to attain a goal.

tip one's hat to   to recognize someone for an accomplishment
related idiom: **hats off to** (congratulations to)
GRAMMAR NOTE: *Hats off to* is usually used to start a sentence.

■ The senior senator from North Carolina **tipped his hat to** the junior senator by
mentioning her accomplishments in his speech.

■ **Hats off to** Andrew for getting the Madison account for our company.

Nice going.   an expression of praise
also: **Way to go.**
GRAMMAR/USAGE NOTES: These idioms are always used as set phrases. They can be used
sarcastically to show the opposite of praise.

■ You got an excellent score on the Scholastic Aptitude Test. **Nice going.**

■ You were selected as a finalist in the modeling contest? **Way to go**, Chris!

■ You locked your keys in your car again? **Nice going!**

pat oneself on the back   to praise oneself

■ I don't mean to **pat myself on the back,** but don't you think I made the right decision?

■ You should **pat yourself on the back** for having the bravery to stop that burglary in
progress. Otherwise, who knows what might have been stolen.

EXERCISES

A.   Fill in each blank with the appropriate form of an idiom from this unit. Some sentences
may have more than one correct answer.

1. You got 95 percent on your chemistry midterm? _____ _____!

2. Thanks for watching my dog while I was gone. I really _____ _____
_____. I'll do the same for you some time.

3. Ellen did a great job on her latest business deal. I've got to _____ _____
_____ her for controlling the negotiations so effectively.

4. For all the success I've achieved in life, I _____ _____ _____ my parents
for starting me off well.

5. _____ _____ the workers' input, we've made changes that have resulted in
increased production and a reduced risk of injury.

6. When Janet had a car accident, she _____ _____ _____ _____ that
she was wearing a seat belt and that her car had airbags.

7. Maybe I shouldn't _____ _____ _____ _____ _____, but don't
you think I handled the argument with the judge well?

8. In his farewell speech, the mayor _____ _____ _____ _____ his
victorious opponent for having run a clean campaign.

B. Choose the statement in the right column that best responds to each question in the left column. Write the appropriate number in the blank.

1. Wasn't it thanks to Lee's hard training that he won the weight-lifting contest?

2. Don't you owe it to Miriam for rescuing your cat from the swimming pool?

3. Way to go, Paul. You were really playing well today, weren't you?

4. Shouldn't we tip our hat to the coach for putting together a championship team?

5. Hats off to the manager for opening the nightclub to us after hours, don't you think?

___ a. We should. We really have to hand it to him for getting us all in shape.

___ b. Yes. He should pat himself on the back for preparing so well.

___ c. I thank my lucky stars that she was nearby when it fell in.

___ d. You can say that again. We really owe him one.

___ e. Yes, and nice going, yourself! You played an excellent game, too.

C. Use the idioms in your spoken or written answers to the following questions.

1. When was the last time you *counted your lucky stars* after a dangerous situation? Explain what happened.

2. Would you *owe it to* someone who found your wallet and returned it? What might you do in return?

3. When was the last time that you *patted yourself on the back?* What did you accomplish? Explain.

4. Do you *owe someone* big time? What did he or she do for you?

5. Do you think that you have a good life mainly *thanks to* your parents? Why or why not?

D. Using the idioms from this unit or a previous one, develop a presentation about a school awards ceremony. You may want to include the following:

- what the different awards were;
- what the presenters said to praise the different recipients;
- who donated time, money, or equipment to the school;
- who was grateful for their good fortune.

Unit 40
Likes and Dislikes

*__be in the mood for__   to want to do, to desire

USAGE NOTE: This idiom is often used when someone desires a pleasant change from the routines of life.

- I*'m in the mood for* a quiet dinner and maybe a movie, just the two of us. Does that sound good to you?
- Suddenly you*'re in the mood for* a cup of coffee, so you want me to take a break with you?

*__go for__   to enjoy or be attracted by

GRAMMAR NOTE: This idiom is used with the auxiliary *could* or *would.*

- Couldn't you *go for* a nice glass of iced tea on this hot day? It certainly would be refreshing.
- You know what I would *go for* as a vacation? Two weeks on a South Pacific island with nothing to do but soak up the sun!

*__fit the bill__   to be the perfect match, to be the best solution

- A couple of relaxing days at the beach really *fit the bill* this weekend. It was wonderful of you to make the arrangements.
- Ted was desperate for a new tie, and he was glad when he found one in the hotel gift store that *fit the bill.*

*__grow on__   to become more familiar, comfortable, or attractive

- At first the design and color of the new drapes bothered me, and I wanted to exchange them, but with time they've *grown on* me.
- Don't judge Mindy by first impressions. She's a nice person, and I'm sure she'll *grow on* you as you get to know her.

__for the birds__   stupid, foolish, disliked

- Commuting by car is *for the birds.* It makes much more sense to take the train.
- That movie was *for the birds.* Why does Hollywood continue to produce such trash?

&
(=Couldn't care less)

could care less for   not to have an interest in

> USAGE NOTE: This idiom keeps the same meaning even in the negative, which serves to add emphasis.

- I *could care less for* his opinion. He interferes in everyone's affairs and has nothing constructive to offer.
- John *couldn't care less* where they went for brunch, much less what they ate.

turn someone's stomach   to make someone feel sick about something, to disgust

> USAGE NOTE: The meaning of this idiom can include physical discomfort in the abdomen.

- It *turns my stomach* when I think that I caused over a thousand dollars' worth of damage to my car by backing into that pole.
- Seeing a film of doctors doing heart surgery, with all the knives and blood, just *turns my stomach.* I'm sorry if I've managed to *turn your stomach* too.

make someone's skin crawl   to cause a strong negative reaction, both physical and emotional
also: **give someone the creeps**

- Doesn't the thought of a spider on your neck *make your skin crawl?*
- It *gives* me *the creeps* every time I think about the night we spent in that deserted campsite.

EXERCISES

A. Fill in each blank with the appropriate form of an idiom from this unit. Some sentences may have more than one correct answer.   *normal, routine*

1. Oprah and William wanted to escape the (daily grind) so a remote cabin in the mountains really _fit_ _the_ _bill_.

2. I'm thirsty. Could you _go_ _for_ a cold soda?

3. In the beginning, Vera didn't care for the pattern of the new carpet, but gradually it began to _grow_ _on_ her.

4. Whenever I think of all the money I lost in Las Vegas, it _turn_ _my_ _stomach_.

5. Would you _be_ _in_ _the_ _mood_ _for_ a nice stroll under the moonlight? It's a beautiful evening.

6. All this overtime work without extra pay is _for_ _the_ _birds_. I'm going to start refusing to do it!   *game; acting out*

7. Perhaps playing (charades) is appealing to you, but really, Jerry and I _could_ _care_ _less_ _for_ it. Let's play Scrabble instead, OK?

8. The cobwebs caught in my hair _made_ _my_ _skin_ _crawl_ as I imagined spiders in them.

125

B. Choose the statement in the right column that best responds to each question in the left column. Write the appropriate number in the blank.

1. Isn't this cold, wet weather for the birds?

2. Wouldn't a nice nap on the lawn fit the bill right now?

3. What kind of dessert are you in the mood for?

4. Didn't the sight of the dead animal in the forest turn your stomach?

5. Doesn't the thought of someone peering in the window make your skin crawl?

_5_ a. Seeing a stranger looking in would give anyone the creeps.

_1_ b. I don't know. I think the rainy season has grown on me.

_2_ c. You could care less for resting. You just don't want to (mow) the grass! — cut

_3_ d. I could go for a frosty ice-cream shake!

_4_ e. I'll say. The bugs crawling over the body gave me the creeps, too.

C. Use the idioms in your spoken or written answers to the following questions.

1. What kind of vacation would **fit the bill** for you right now?

2. Do you **go for** dangerous activities such as snowboarding or skydiving? Why or why not?

3. When might you **be in the mood for** some time alone? Use your imagination.

4. What things in life are **for the birds?** Why?

5. What foods **could** you **care less for?** What don't you like about them?

D. Using the idioms from this unit or a previous one, tell a classmate about a real or imaginary trip to an unusual place. You may want to include the following:

- what made the trip perfect for you;
- what you did for pleasure;
- what you had no interest in or actually disliked;
- whether anything happened to make you want to leave;
- how you felt after you'd been there for a while.

Review: Units 31–40

A. **Circle the expression that best completes each sentence.**

1. Susan asked a neighbor to _____ her children when she went to the doctor's office.
   a. pitch in
   b. look after
   c. come along

2. Why do I constantly have to _____ you about doing the yard work?
   a. keep after
   b. leave to
   c. grow on

3. When Matthew is being pressured unfairly, he certainly can _____.
   a. thank his lucky stars
   b. turn my stomach
   c. stand his ground

4. How could Elaine have possibly recommended this restaurant to us? It certainly was _____.
   a. a bum steer
   b. a pep talk
   c. an acid test

5. At first Luke and his friend disagreed with each other, but after further discussion they _____
   a. were dead set against
   b. took shape
   c. saw eye to eye

6. I don't care for this movie. It's really _____.
   a. for the birds
   b. on my second wind
   c. on a roll

7. We've got to _____ Yolanda for making the effort to control her anger, even though she doesn't always succeed.
   a. follow up on
   b. hand it to
   c. see about

8. The politician's family tried to _____ running for governor, but she wouldn't consider their arguments.
   a. gain ground on
   b. come out for
   c. talk her into

9. The struggling athlete didn't think he could _____ the other runners, but suddenly he felt stronger and caught up.
   a. keep up with
   b. go for
   c. side with

10. Even though the research is going slowly, the scientist _____ on the laboratory phase of the work.
    a. is taking a stand
    b. is making headway
    c. is backing up

B. **Indicate whether each statement is TRUE (T) or FALSE (F).**

_____ 1. If you have set your sights on a promotion, you might go overboard in your work.

_____ 2. Someone who is stubborn as a mule would give in to your request readily.

_____ 3. A political cause would gain steam if a lot of people jumped on the bandwagon.

_____ 4. If two people were having a war of words, they'd be on the same wavelength.

_____ 5. You would definitely be in the mood for something that made your skin crawl.

_____ 6. Someone who was falling behind in school might need a shot in the arm.

_____ 7. If your boss dumped work on you, you might not want to see it through.

_____ 8. Words of wisdom might bring someone around to your way of thinking.

_____ 9. You would stand behind the arguments of someone who didn't have a leg to stand on.

_____ 10. If you steered someone straight, you might give yourself a pat on the back.

127

C. Complete the puzzle with the missing parts of the idioms in the sentences below.

ACROSS

1. Did Paul _____ on the job of organizing the party?
7. I'd like to _____ to the manager about the matter.
8. The police officer needed _____ in the emergency.
9. _____ to you, we made the right choice of car.
10. Henry doesn't carry his _____ at the office.
11. Spider webs give me the _____ .
14. We shouldn't be at _____ with each other.
17. The elderly man took the lost dog under his _____ .
18. Lisa gave it her best _____ on the final exam.

DOWN

2. Eventually she came _____ to my way of thinking.
3. Nancy could care _____ for exercise of any kind.
4. Bob stuck to his _____ and did it his way.
5. The clerk checked the _____ trail carefully.
6. Did the fans _____ the team on to victory?
8. I'll stand _____ you 100 percent.
12. A _____-headed attitude won't get you anywhere.
13. You did a great job. Nice _____ !
15. Vera counted her lucky _____ after the accident.
16. I appreciated your _____-up on the problem.
17. It's not right that you always get your _____ .

Unit 41
Knowledge and Perception

hear of to know about, to have received information on
> GRAMMAR NOTE: This idiom is usually used with the present perfect or past perfect tense.
> - I've never *heard of* a retail chain called Melville's. It's supposedly big in the Midwest. Have you ever *heard of* it?
> - Susan was very interested in buying this obscure version of her favorite opera because she'd never *heard of* it before.

be news to to be a surprising piece of new information
> - It *is news to* me that there was a powerful earthquake in Thailand earlier today. I haven't opened the paper yet.
> - The regulation preventing completion of the housing addition *was news to* the building inspector. She's going to have to check with her supervisor.

know-how knowledge, skill
> USAGE NOTE: This idiom refers to knowledge or skill required to make things.
> - The armed forces have used all their *know-how* to build a defense system against laser-guided weaponry.
> - This self-paced tutorial provides you with all the *know-how* to select materials and build a garden trellis yourself.

broaden one's horizons to expand one's knowledge and abilities
> - Students are expected to *broaden their horizons* by studying a variety of subjects in high school and college.
> - To *broaden her horizons,* the girl from a city in New Jersey went to stay on a sheep farm outside of London.

pick up to learn easily
> GRAMMAR NOTE: This idiom is separable.
> - Todd never has to study his notes much. He just *picks up* the necessary information during the lectures.
> - Julio has always had an easy time learning languages. He seems to *pick* them *up* quickly.

through the grapevine   from friends and other informal sources

- I heard *through the grapevine* that there was a multimedia technician job opening at the library.
- News of the unexpected court decision spread *through the grapevine* and was the talk of the evening.

get wind of   to learn about something important or secret

- What will happen if the boss *gets wind of* the big farewell party we had for Ophelia in the conference room?
- When Mom *gets wind of* the problems you've been causing your teachers, you'll be in big trouble.

in the loop   involved in or knowledgeable about
opposite meaning: **out of the loop**
USAGE NOTE: The first idiom is used for people who are involved in the decision-making process.

- Brian felt a lot of responsibility because he was *in the loop* on all operational decisions at the maximum-security prison.
- The lower-level managers were *out of the loop* about proposed cuts in the workforce.

make of   to discern, to perceive
GRAMMAR/USAGE NOTES: This idiom is usually used in a question or noun phrase starting with *what*.

- That was a very unusual TV documentary. What did you *make of* it?
- When Uncle Otto saw the noise and commotion in the family room, he didn't know what to *make of* it.

EXERCISES

A.   Fill in each blank with the appropriate form of an idiom from this unit.

1. Joel took an extension course in woodworking at the local community college because he wanted to _____ _____ _____.

2. Have you ever _____ _____ an island called Kiawah? It's supposed to be somewhere along the coast of South Carolina.

3. Even though Sandy started playing piano at a late age, she has _____ it _____ very quickly and is now quite proficient.

4. I thought that the movie was quite unusual but that the ending didn't fit the story. So what did you _____ _____ it?

5. We haven't been able to fix this door ourselves, so let's hire someone who has the _____ - _____ to do it right.

6. The doctor became very upset when she _____ _____ _____ the rumor about her that was circulating the hospital.

7. The investor hadn't read the newspaper yet, so the big drop in stock prices _____ _____ _____ him.

8. I heard _____ _____ _____ that some employees may be laid off due to budget problems.

9. I'll ask Joel about the rumor. He's always _____ _____ _____ regarding the latest developments in our company.

B. Choose the statement in the right column that best responds to each question in the left column. Write the appropriate number in the blank.

1. What do you make of the noise coming from the engine?

2. How did Bob get wind of the big changes in management?

3. I heard through the grapevine that the school dance was canceled. Did you hear the same rumor?

4. Is Kay taking a Spanish course in order to broaden her horizons?

5. Have you heard of the city's plan to redevelop our neighborhood?

____ a. No, I didn't. I'm out of the loop on campus these days.

____ b. No, I haven't. Such a plan is news to me.

____ c. I have no idea. I don't have any know-how about motors.

____ d. You know how he's always in the loop about these things.

____ e. Yes. She thinks she'll pick up the language quickly.

C. Use the idioms in your spoken or written answers to the following questions.

1. Do you have the *know-how* to repair things around your home, such as electrical and plumbing fixtures? Why or why not?

2. What place hadn't you *heard of* until quite recently? How did you learn about it?

3. Do you *pick up* languages easily? Why or why not?

4. What do you *make of* all the violence in the world? What can be done about it, if anything?

5. Are you interested in *broadening your horizons?* In what ways?

C. Using the idioms from this unit or a previous one, develop a dialogue or role play involving two people discussing a newly opened trade school or college. You may want to include the following:

- who knows about the school and who doesn't;
- what trade or subject one of the people wants to study;
- why the person wants to pursue that trade or subject;
- whether anything about the school is surprising.

Unit 42
Thought and Reconsideration

think over   to consider carefully
also: **give thought (to)**

GRAMMAR/USAGE NOTES: These idioms are separable and are used when someone needs time to think before making a decision. *Thought* can be preceded by words such as *more, some,* or *enough.*

- When Jerry asked Ms. Jenkins for a raise, she said that she would *think* it *over.*
- The judge agreed to *give* the matter some *thought* before rendering his verdict in the morning.
- Do you think that you *gave* enough *thought to* the matter before you decided?

think through   to analyze in a logical way

GRAMMAR NOTE: This idiom is separable.

- There must be a solution to this math problem. I've just got to *think through* the process more carefully.
- Noreen still wasn't sure which business internship to accept, so she spent another weekend *thinking* it *through* with her parents.

take into consideration   to consider as one factor in a situation
also: **take into account**

GRAMMAR NOTE: These idioms require an object after the verb *take.*

- The school board *took* the student's fine academic record *into consideration* when it voted for only a three-day suspension from school after the fighting incident.
- Did you *take* the refund *into account* when you figured the total amount due?

sleep on it   to consider a situation overnight

- This matter is too important to settle right now. Let me *sleep on it* and let you know in the morning.
- Don't rush your decision just because you feel pressure from others. It would be best to *sleep on it* further.

food for thought   something that is well worth considering

- I think you should listen to what your counselor said about a balance between work and school. It was good *food for thought,* in my opinion.
- The lecture offered a lot of *food for thought* regarding the effects of pollution on the environment.

have second thoughts   to reconsider, to doubt one's initial decision
also: think twice

USAGE NOTE: These expressions are often followed by *about* and a gerund phrase.

■ I would *have second thoughts* about hiring a security firm to put alarms in my house unless I had checked its references very carefully.

■ Because of his fear of heights, Lawrence *thought twice* about riding on the rollercoaster, but finally he decided to brave it.

go back and forth (on)   to constantly change one's opinion or position

GRAMMAR NOTE: This idiom often becomes a gerund following the verb *keep*.

■ Sheila doesn't know why she *goes back and forth on* the right style of wedding dress. She prefers a traditional look, but her friends are urging a more modern one.

■ Don't keep *going back and forth* about what to order for dinner. Steak is always your final choice anyway.

take back   to withdraw what one says, to retract a statement

GRAMMAR NOTE: This idiom is separable.

■ Shouldn't you *take back* what you said about his new jacket? Actually, I think it looks very nice.

■ I've got to *take* that *back*—you're not *one* of the funniest people I know, you are *the* funniest!

EXERCISES

A.   Fill in each blank with the appropriate form of an idiom from this unit. Some sentences may have more than one correct answer.

LUIS: Hi, Julie. What are you working on?

JULIE: My physics project. I'm _____ _____ _____ about the topic I first
  chose.
  ₁

LUIS: How so?

JULIE: It seems so dry and boring. I keep _____ _____ _____ _____
  on doing it or changing to a more practical application.
  ₂

LUIS: Practical projects are sometimes more interesting—I _____ that
  ₃
  _____—they're *always* more interesting, and the professors seem to prefer
  them too.

JULIE: You know, that's good _____ _____ _____. Thanks for the advice.
  ₄

LUIS: No problem. Now, have you had a chance to _____ _____ my friend's
  ₅
  invitation to play soccer for the Rebels club? You said you needed to _____
  ₆
  _____ _____ for a while.

JULIE: I'm still concerned that playing competitive soccer will affect my studies.

LUIS: Oh, you can do both. You know how much you enjoy soccer.

(continued on next page)

JULIE: It's a great sport. Well, can I have some more time to _____ it _____?
7

LUIS: Of course. And don't forget to _____ _____ _____ that the usual
8

fees will be waived for you.

JULIE: I know. That's an attractive offer. I'll let you know soon.

LUIS: I can't ask for more!

B. Choose the statement in the right column that best responds to each question in the left column. Write the appropriate number in the blank.

1. Is Leah still going back and forth on whether to accept the job transfer to Europe?

2. Did Gail take into account the cost of insuring and maintaining a new car?

3. Has Henry taken back what he said to his boss about his job?

4. Doesn't the high risk factor make you think twice about doing stunt work?

5. Did you think over my idea of starting a company together?

____ a. No. That's why she's having second thoughts about buying one.

____ b. Yes, I did. It's interesting food for thought, at the very least.

____ c. Yes, she's taking plenty of time to think the move through.

____ d. I've taken it into consideration, but it really doesn't scare me.

____ e. Yes, he has. He should have given it more thought before speaking.

C. Use the idioms in your spoken or written answers to the following questions.

1. What would you have to *take into consideration* if you were to make a major purchase such as a car or house?

2. Does the expression "You only live once" offer you any *food for thought?* Explain.

3. Would you *think twice* about riding in a hot-air balloon? Why or why not?

4. What was the last decision that you *went back and forth on?* What did you finally decide?

5. Have you ever made an unfair or unkind comment that you had to *take back?* What was it?

D. Using the idioms from this unit or a previous one, tell a classmate about a time when you had to make an important decision. You may want to include the following:

- what the situation or problem was;
- what factors you considered before deciding;
- what advice other people gave you;
- any uncertainty you might have had;
- how long it took you to decide;
- what the final decision was.

Unit 43
Noticing and Realizing

stand out   to be obvious, to be noticeable
also: **stick out**

Usage Notes: These idioms are used when something is quite different, sometimes in a negative way, from other things around it. The phrase *like a sore thumb* can be added to *stick out*.

■ The little girl sitting on her father's shoulders **stood out** in the crowd of people watching the magician perform.

■ If you wear shorts and a T-shirt to the beach on a cold, cloudy day like this, you'll **stick out** like a sore thumb.

catch someone's eye   to attract someone's attention

■ A beautiful dress in the window of a department store **caught Tracy's eye.**

■ When the manager looked out the back window of the store, something unusual **caught his eye,** so he called 911 for the police to investigate.

pay attention (to)   to concentrate on, to listen to

■ The tour guide got upset at the children for not **paying attention** during the visit to the museum.

■ The businessman **paid attention to** his accountant's advice to put more of his money into tax-sheltered investments.

take note (of)   to make an effort to notice or observe

■ When the lecturer indicated she was going to finish by summarizing the ten basic steps to success as a writer, everyone in the audience **took note.**

■ Did you **take note of** the way the coach was holding the tennis racket when she demonstrated proper forehand technique?

look out (for)   to be ready to notice potential danger

Grammar Note: This idiom is often used in a command form.

■ Every time I walk under those trees I **look out for** falling branches. Just the other day someone was injured by one.

■ **Look out!** You almost walked in front of the truck that just barreled by.

ring a bell   to be familiar as something one has noticed before

■ The name Ollie Carl **rings a bell.** Isn't he the carpenter who built our storage shed?

■ The street name Adams Avenue doesn't **ring a bell** to me. Are you sure it's in this neighborhood?

dawn on   to understand or realize something unexpectedly
also: **occur to, cross one's mind**

USAGE NOTE: This idiom often starts with the subject pronoun *it* and is used with adverbs such as *suddenly* and *just*.

- The solution to the math problem suddenly **dawned on** Julie after she had spent over a half hour working on it.
- On the way to work, it **occurred to** Jim that he'd forgotten to lock the front door of his apartment.
- It just **crossed my mind** that we forgot to mail Aunt Ruth a birthday card this year. We'll have to write her a note of apology.

sink in   to become understandable or meaningful to someone

- No matter how many times I teach students the meaning of some words, it just never seems to *sink in.*
- It took a long time before the significance of the announcement *sank in* among those gathered in the conference room.

EXERCISES

A.   Fill in each blank with the appropriate form of an idiom from this unit. Some sentences may have more than one correct answer.

1. Somehow the name Donna Montgomery _____ _____ _____. Could she have gone to our high school?

2. Why are you wearing that striped purple shirt? It really _____ _____ against your white pants.

3. Children, stop talking to each other and _____ _____ _____ the lesson.

4. The best solution to the scheduling problem suddenly _____ _____ Martin as he was shopping for a tie.

5. As the electrician replaced the light switch, I _____ _____ _____ the way he did it so that I would know how to do it myself.

6. Barbara was about to drive her car through the intersection when the flashing red light of a fire truck _____ _____ _____.

7. That lawn may look good enough for playing ball, but you'll constantly have to _____ _____ _____ gopher holes. They can be dangerous.

8. The Madisons were quick to get married, but the full significance didn't _____ _____ until later.

B. Choose the statement in the right column that best responds to each question in the left column. Write the appropriate number in the blank.

1. Doesn't the huge hat that woman's wearing really stick out?
2. When will Victor realize he has to look out for snakes in the grass?
3. Does the name Jesse Owens ring a bell to you?
4. Coach, what did you just tell me to pay attention to?
5. Has it occurred to you that winning a million dollars means we can both quit our jobs?

____ a. I don't think it will dawn on him until he gets bitten!

____ b. It sure does. The size is what first caught my eye.

____ c. No, it hasn't. The full impact hasn't sunk in yet!

____ d. He was an exceptional athlete who stood out in the 1930s.

____ e. I told you to take note of the proper way to hold the hockey stick.

C. Use the idioms in your spoken or written answers to the following questions.

1. What in your home *sticks out?* Is it good or bad?
2. What should you *look out for* while driving?
3. When you're shopping in a department store, what kinds of things *catch your eye?*
4. Has it *dawned on* you that computers may be taking over our lives? What might be done about it, if anything?
5. Has it *occurred to* you that world affairs might be spinning out of control? What, if anything, might be done about that?

D. Using the idioms from this unit or a previous one, develop a presentation about a real or imagined day at an amusement park, carnival, or festival. You may want to include the following:

- what you did;
- what you noticed during the day;
- whether there was anything dangerous;
- how you felt when you got on a scary ride or participated in an event.

Unit 44
Logic and Illogic

stand to reason   to be a logical consequence

GRAMMAR NOTE: This idiom usually occurs with the subject pronoun *it* and is followed by a *that* clause.

- If you're qualified and well-received by the interviewing committee, it *stands to reason* that you'll get the job.
- It *stands to reason* that a person of her integrity would resent the unfair criticism of those who oppose her political views.

go without saying   to be obvious without being mentioned

GRAMMAR NOTE: This idiom usually occurs with the subject pronoun *it* and is followed by a *that* clause.

- It *goes without saying* that this has been the warmest winter we've had in years. I wonder if cold weather will ever arrive.
- "Time flies" is an expression whose meaning *goes without saying,* especially as one grows older.

put two and two together   to draw conclusions from available information, to deduce

USAGE NOTE: No number other than *two* can be used.

- Seeing the cookie crumbs on the floor and her son grinning sheepishly at her, Troy's mother could easily *put two and two together.*
- The federal agents quickly solved the crime by analyzing the evidence and *putting two and two together.*

jump to conclusions   to assume or conclude something prematurely

USAGE NOTE: This idiom is used when someone doesn't have or isn't considering all the facts and may be making a mistake.

- Kate *jumped to conclusions* when she saw sun in the morning, but by noon it was raining heavily and she had not brought her umbrella.
- You haven't heard Greg's explanation of what happened, so you shouldn't *jump to conclusions.*

hare-brained   foolish, irrational

- I've heard all kinds of excuses for people being late, but the one about the man whose pants supposedly got stuck in the elevator is as **hare-brained** as they get!
- What kind of **hare-brained** plan has Brian created for us this weekend? The last one almost put us in the hospital!

no rhyme or reason   without any common sense or purpose
also: **neither rhyme nor reason, without rhyme or reason**
USAGE NOTE: These idioms either follow *there* and a form of the verb *be,* or they follow the verb *have.*

- There was **no rhyme or reason** to her argument, even though many of her supporters were nodding their heads in agreement.
- The tennis player's loud complaints during the match had **neither rhyme nor reason,** so the referee was forced to reprimand him.
- You never seem to watch any one TV show for more than five minutes. Actually, you're usually just turning the channels **without rhyme or reason!**

put the cart before the horse   to be illogical, to be done in the wrong order
USAGE NOTE: This idiom is used when a person places something that is second in importance before something that logically should be first.

- Harold **put the cart before the horse** when he made deposits on hotel reservations before he had purchased his airline tickets.
- Buying a new car before you've actually gotten a raise seems to be **putting the cart before the horse.**

pie in the sky   an impossible dream or expectation

- Yvette's dream of starting her own business is **pie in the sky** to me. She doesn't have the education or experience.
- It may be **pie in the sky** to think that some day all people will live in peace, harmony, and prosperity.

EXERCISES

A.   Fill in each blank with the appropriate form of an idiom from this unit. Some sentences may have more than one correct answer.

1. Why would someone rob a homeless person of only a few dollars? There's _____ _____ _____ _____ to such an action.

2. Buying computer hardware before knowing what software you want to use is _____ _____ _____ _____ _____ _____.

3. Louise spends ten dollars a week on lottery tickets, hoping to get rich. That's just _____ _____ _____ _____, if you ask me.

4. Have you heard the _____ - _____ scheme that Timothy is suggesting? He wants us to invest in a thoroughbred race horse together!

5. Just because your neighbor was nearby when your car got dented doesn't mean he did it. You shouldn't _____ _____ _____.

6. When none of her friends mentioned her birthday at all, Jane _____ _____ _____ _____ _____ and realized that there was going to be a surprise party.

(continued on next page)

7. It _____ _____ _____ that it's better to tell the truth than to lie in most situations.

8. It _____ _____ _____ that a truthful person receives more respect than one who practices deceit.

B. Choose the statement in the right column that best responds to each question in the left column. Write the appropriate number in the blank.

1. Is it just pie in the sky for Allen to think he can make the Olympic swim team?

2. Was there any rhyme or reason to Donald's objections to our plan?

3. Aren't you jumping to conclusions when you say that Bonnie made that terrible decision?

4. How does Maryanne think of such hare-brained ways to make money?

5. Doesn't it stand to reason that we should read the instructions before we put the stereo system together?

____ a. No. In my opinion, he jumped to conclusions and objected without thinking.

____ b. It goes without saying that at forty he's too old to compete.

____ c. I don't know. Her schemes have neither rhyme nor reason.

____ d. I'm just putting two and two together when I blame her.

____ e. Of course. Otherwise, we'd be putting the cart before the horse.

C. Use the idioms in your spoken or written answers to the following questions.

1. What are some things that *go without saying* when you're trying to learn another language?

2. What was the last *hare-brained* plan or activity that you were involved in? What happened?

3. Does it *stand to reason* that a person who is caught stealing should go to jail? Why or why not?

4. If you had a dream for the future that everyone told you was *pie in the sky,* would you pursue it anyway? Why or why not?

5. Try to think of a time when you *put the cart before the horse.* What happened?

D. Using the idioms from this unit or a previous one, develop a dialogue or role play about two people who are discussing the actions of a mutual friend. You may want to include the following:

- what problem or situation the friend is involved in;
- the logical or illogical actions of the friend;
- general comments or opinions about the friend;
- how the two people form their opinions.

Unit 45
Expressing Oneself

speak one's mind   to express one's ideas or opinions

USAGE NOTE: This idiom is used when someone has strong opinions, or when someone waits for the best time to express his or her thoughts.

- The unhappy stockholders had a chance to *speak their minds* at the special meeting held to discuss devastating financial losses for the company.
- It wasn't until everyone else had expressed themselves that Woodrow carefully *spoke his mind.*

fire away   to ask whatever question one wants

USAGE NOTE: This idiom is used when a person is being evaluated or questioned for some reason.

- I have nothing to hide about my past. *Fire away!*
- The spokesperson first assured the press that she would answer all questions and then let them *fire away* for over an hour.

blurt out   to express an idea or feeling without thought, to speak unintentionally

- The game-show contestant suddenly *blurted out* the wrong answer and made everyone laugh.
- Later Fabio had to apologize for the angry words he had *blurted out* during a disagreement with his friend.

have a way with words   to express oneself well, to communicate effectively
also: **have a gift for gab**

- Robert really *has a way with words,* doesn't he? There's always a group of people around him listening to his insightful comments!
- Sybille became a comedian because she *has* a real *gift for gab.* Ever since she was a little girl she's been entertaining people with jokes.

beat around the bush   to not deal directly with a problem

USAGE NOTE: In the negative, this idiom means that a problem is directly addressed.

- Janine *beat around the bush* and offered one excuse after another for not being able to make my party.
- Let's not *beat around the bush.* You can't stand it here, and I love it. So why don't you leave and I'll stay?

clam up   to suddenly refuse to speak

    USAGE NOTE: This idiom is used when someone has cause to stop talking, such as a threat of punishment.

- Dorothy is quick to criticize others and expect a response, but when she receives criticism, she just *clams up.*
- Government officials involved in legislation to restrict tobacco advertising *clammed up* when industry lobbyists threatened to sue.

shut up   to stop talking

    GRAMMAR/USAGE NOTES: This idiom is often used in a command form and only in very informal situations with close friends and family.

- *Shut up,* Ed. Can't you leave the room and let me work in peace?
- Every time I tease my little brother about his teddy bear collection, he tells me to *shut up.*

hold down   to talk more softly

    GRAMMAR/USAGE NOTES: This idiom is separable and used with nouns such as *noise* and with the pronoun *it.*

- The man at the microphone had trouble *holding down* the noise in the hot, crowded auditorium.
- The baby is trying to sleep in the corner of the room. Could you please try to *hold* it *down?*

the cat has one's tongue   to be unable to speak, not to know what to say
    also: **Cat got your tongue?**

    USAGE NOTE: This idiom is used when someone cannot express himself or herself momentarily, either by not knowing what to say or not having anything suitable to say.

- That's the first time I've ever seen Jacqueline at a loss for words. I wonder why the *cat had her tongue.*
- What's the matter? *Cat got your tongue?* I asked you a simple question—Where were you last night?

EXERCISES

A.   Fill in each blank with the appropriate form of an idiom from this unit. Some sentences may have more than one correct answer.

1. Could you please _____ _____ your conversation? It's disturbing the library patrons.

2. Without thinking, the teenage boy _____ _____ his opinion of his girlfriend's new hat.

3. I asked you a direct question and you didn't answer me. What's the matter—does _____ _____ _____ _____ _____?

4. Jennifer is a very opinionated person. She never hesitates to _____ _____ _____.

5. After the president had finished his speech, he invited the reporters to _____ _____ with questions.

6. Isn't the talk show host quite articulate when she expresses herself? She really _____ _____ _____ _____ _____.

7. When Lisa's little brother started reading aloud from his book, Lisa impolitely told him to _____ _____.

8. The students were actively talking together, but when the teacher entered the room, they _____ _____.

9. You're not answering my question directly. Please don't _____ _____ _____ _____ like that.

B. Choose the statement in the right column that best responds to each question in the left column. Write the appropriate number in the blank.

1. Should I ask the children to hold it down in the other room?

____ a. Yes, she did, but when asked about personal issues, she just clammed up.

2. Steven has a way with words, doesn't he?

____ b. No, I'm just being careful not to blurt out the wrong thing.

3. What's the matter—cat got your tongue?

____ c. What I'd really like them to do is shut up!

4. Why are you beating around the bush about the problem?

____ d. He sure does. He really has a gift for gab.

5. Did the mayoral candidate let the audience fire away during the question-and-answer period?

____ e. Because I'm afraid you won't like it if I really speak my mind.

C. Use the idioms in your spoken or written answers to the following questions.

1. Are you comfortable *speaking your mind* in English? Why or why not?

2. In what kind of situation are you most likely to *clam up?* Try to think of specific examples.

3. When might you tell a friend or family member to *shut up?*

4. For what reasons might you choose to *beat around the bush* instead of answering a question directly?

5. What can be the problem with *blurting out* one's thoughts and feelings? Does this ever happen to you?

D. Using the idioms from this unit or a previous one, develop a presentation about a real or imagined discussion in class. You may want to include the following:

- the topic of the class discussion;
- who communicated well;
- who spoke without thinking;
- who needed to express himself or herself more;
- who should have been more quiet.

Unit 46
Decisions and Choices

rule of thumb   a general rule, a practical guideline

USAGE NOTE: This idiom is used in judging the best course of action to take.

- The writer's **rule of thumb** is to capture the reader's imagination and interest in the first few lines of prose.

- As a **rule of thumb,** never attach a major appliance to an electrical outlet without first making sure it's properly grounded.

pros and cons   factors to consider both in favor of and against something

USAGE NOTE: This idiom often follows the verb *weigh* or *consider.*

- The grand jury weighed all the **pros and cons** in the case and agreed to indict the county administrator after only three hours of deliberation.

- Have you considered all the **pros and cons** of buying a home instead of a condominium?

leave up to   to give someone the responsibility of acting or deciding
related idiom: **be up to** (to have the responsibility of acting or deciding)

GRAMMAR/USAGE NOTES: An object is placed after the verb *leave.* Adverbs such as *completely* can be placed in the middle of both idioms.

- Nobody is as good as Heather at organizing fund-raising events. We should **leave** it **up to** her to form the committee and make all the arrangements.

- The decision about where to go during spring break **is** completely **up to** you. I'm agreeable to doing anything except staying here.

make up one's mind   to finally reach a decision

GRAMMAR/USAGE NOTES: This idiom is separable and can take a plural form. It is used when someone requires time to make a careful decision. *Up* can come before or after *one's mind.* The adjective *own* sometimes precedes the noun *mind.*

- It's good to see you again, Mr. and Mrs. Curtis. Well, have you **made up your minds** about what car to buy?

- Could you give me another day to think about the contract? I haven't **made my mind up** yet.

- Don't ask me to make that decision for you. You have to **make up your** own **mind.**

leave open   to delay making final arrangements

> GRAMMAR NOTE: This idiom is always separated by an object.

- Even though we know that the meeting will be on August 23, we'll have to *leave* the time *open* for now.
- I'd love to go with you, but I'll have to check my calendar first. Can we *leave* it *open,* and I'll let you know later?

call the shots   to be the person who makes the decision or choice

- Don't look to me for a decision on that issue. It's Norman who's *calling the shots.*
- When emergency crews arrived from several districts, it was the home-district supervisor who *called the shots* at the chemical plant explosion.

settle on   to finally choose

- I checked the quality and price of several coats and finally *settled on* a gray suede and leather flight jacket.
- After considering many parts of the United States, the Iacoccas *settled on* California as the best place to raise a family.

take one's pick   to make whatever choice one wants

> GRAMMAR NOTE: This idiom often occurs in a command form.

- Our dog Melissa just had a litter of four female and two male puppies. If you'd like a pet, you can *take your pick.*
- There are plenty of empty seats all over the auditorium. *Take your pick.*

take it or leave it   either to choose something or not to choose it

> GRAMMAR/USAGE NOTES: This idiom is used to indicate strongly that there is only one choice. It is used informally and often as a command preceded by *either.*

- There's nothing else for dinner except pasta and vegetables, so *take it or leave it!*
- Sir, I can't keep the other people waiting in line any longer. This is the only flight we have available. Either *take it or leave it,* please!

EXERCISES

A.   Fill in each blank with the appropriate form of an idiom from this unit.

I.

LOA: Burt, do you want to eat out tonight?

BURT: I don't care. I'll _____ it _____ _____ you to decide.
                        1

LOA: Come on, Burt. I'm asking you because I can't _____ _____ _____
                                                                       2

   own _____.

BURT: OK, then let's eat here. What's for dinner?

LOA: Look in the freezer and _____ _____ _____.
                                           3

BURT: Pick what? The only edible thing in here is a frozen pizza. I don't feel like that.

LOA: That's all we've got, so _____ _____ _____ _____ _____!
                                           4

BURT: Well, when you put it that way, I guess we have no choice but to eat out!

(continued on next page)

II.   The Andersons are weighing the _____ _____ _____ of
purchasing a new vehicle versus fixing up their old one. Mrs. Anderson, who
usually _____ _____ _____ on major purchases, wants to buy a new
car because their old one will soon need major repairs. Mr. Anderson, on the
other hand, prefers to _____ the decision _____ until they can compare
the relative costs more thoroughly. The Andersons have finally _____
_____ checking with their local dealer to see what the _____ _____
_____ is in such cases.

B.   Choose the statement in the right column that best responds to each question in the left column. Write the appropriate number in the blank.

1. Have you made up your mind about settling in Oregon when you retire?

2. Who calls the shots in your family—you or your wife?

3. Can't we leave the day and time of the appointment open for now?

4. Is it up to me to decide which ride we take first at Disneyland?

5. What is your rule of thumb on the time you spend on homework each night?

____ a. Sure. It doesn't matter where we start, so take your pick.

____ b. Not yet. We're still weighing the pros and cons of moving.

____ c. Well, I've settled on about an hour of work each evening.

____ d. I generally leave important decisions up to her.

____ e. Sorry, only Friday morning is free. Take it or leave it!

C.   Use the idioms in your spoken or written answers to the following questions.

1. Who usually **calls the shots** in your family? Why?
2. What decisions might your parents or friends **leave up to** you?
3. What are the **pros and cons** of studying in a country other than your own?
4. Tell about a time when you had trouble **making up your mind.** What happened?
5. What are some **rules of thumb** when you have to write an essay?

D.   Using the idioms from this unit or a previous one, develop a dialogue or role play involving two people who are making an important decision. You may want to include the following:

- what they're trying to decide;
- what factors they're considering;
- who usually makes the decision;
- what the final decision is.

Unit 47
Solving Problems

get to the bottom of   to finally find an explanation for something
also: **get to the heart of**

USAGE NOTE: These idioms are often used with nouns such as *problem* and *matter*.

- The garden nursery had been investigating thefts for some time, but it couldn't **get to the bottom of** the problem until an employee was caught using a truck to steal plants.

- **Getting to the heart of** the matter, it seems that both of you want to live as if you were single people instead of a married couple.

nip in the bud   to stop something before it becomes a problem

GRAMMAR NOTE: An object can follow the verb *nip*.

- Athletes should watch for signs of muscle fatigue so that potential injuries can be **nipped in the bud.**

- Stories about the actor's temper were being exaggerated in the Hollywood press, so the actor's agent tried to **nip** the rumors **in the bud.**

wrack one's brains   to think very hard about something (often the solution to a problem)
also: **beat one's brains**

GRAMMAR NOTES: These idioms are usually followed by a gerund phrase, often starting with the verb *try*. The noun *brains* is always plural, even when a single person is involved.

- The fire department workers **wracked their brains** trying to find a way to rescue the kitten from the clogged sewer line.

- I've **beaten my brains** for hours looking for a solution to your dilemma, but I can't think of a good one.

Two heads are better than one.   Two people can find a solution better than one person can alone.

- We can resolve this situation together if we focus all our energies on it. After all, **two heads are better than one.**

- **Two heads are better than one** when a project can best be accomplished through teamwork.

work out   to resolve a problem, to reach an agreement
also: **iron out**

GRAMMAR NOTE: These transitive idioms are separable.

- The nightclub *worked out* an arrangement with nearby homeowners to restrict noise levels after 10:00 P.M.

- There are only a few small matters to *iron out* before we sign the contract. Don't you think we can *iron* them *out* in the next hour or so?

do the trick   to have the desired result, to be an adequate solution

- At first Ellen couldn't move the stuck doorknob, but spraying some lubricant oil inside the mechanism *did the trick.*

- This package should be secured with special strapping tape, but masking tape should *do the trick* for now.

quick fix   a simple, temporary solution to a problem

USAGE NOTE: This idiom is used when it is known that the solution is not the best possible one.

- Using a piece of chewing gum to keep the small part from falling off was a *quick fix* that worked for a while.

- Selling some unused property was a *quick fix* chosen by company directors to avoid declaring bankruptcy.

take a different tack   to approach a problem or situation from a different angle

USAGE NOTE: Adverbs such as *completely* or *somewhat* can be added before the adjective.

- I'm not getting anywhere trying to explain the problem to you. Let me start over and *take a* somewhat *different tack.*

- The marketing company realized that its approach to selling the product wasn't working, so it quickly decided to *take a different tack.*

as a last resort   as the last solution (often the least desirable one)

- If we can't make flight arrangements at this late date, *as a last resort* we'll have to drive for ten hours to get there.

- The doctors think they can treat the ailment with medication, so they'll perform surgery only *as a last resort.*

no magic bullet   no complete solution or cure to a problem

- Scientists have discovered *no magic bullet* for cancer, even though they are getting much closer to understanding how it functions.

- Lowering interest rates is *no magic bullet,* but it should help to stimulate the economy.

EXERCISES

A.   Fill in each blank with the appropriate form of an idiom from this unit. Some sentences may have more than one correct answer.

1. Julio much prefers taking a direct nonstop flight to Atlanta, but he's willing to transfer planes in St. Louis _____ _____ _____ _____.

2. Would a piece of wire holding the exhaust pipe to the frame of the car be a _____ _____ until we can find a repair shop?

3. This approach to the situation isn't getting us anywhere, so let's _____ _____ _____ _____.

4. For days Nora has _____ _____ _____ trying to find a good topic for her doctoral thesis, but she's rejected every idea so far.

5. I really appreciate your assistance in this matter. As the saying goes, _____ _____ _____ _____ _____ _____.

6. Our boys are starting to watch too much television again. We'd better _____ it _____ _____ _____ before they become addicted.

7. The cracked window needs to be replaced, but clear wrapping tape will _____ _____ _____ for now.

8. The paralyzed mountaineer will probably not be able to walk again because there's still _____ _____ _____ for serious spinal injuries.

9. Two employees had not been talking to each other for days, so the manager brought them together to _____ _____ _____ _____ _____ their problem.

10. After two hours of serious discussion, the two students were able to _____ their problems _____ with the counselor's help.

B. Choose the statement in the right column that best responds to each question in the left column. Write the appropriate number in the blank.

1. Could you help me work out this difficult math question?

2. Will Elaine visit the cancer specialist in Europe as a last resort?

3. Did a serious talk with your daughter about her schoolwork do the trick?

4. How long did they wrack their brains to find a solution to the problem?

5. Did the technician get to the bottom of the problem with the computer?

____ a. Yes, I think we'll be able to nip her bad grades in the bud.

____ b. No, but reinstalling the program was a quick fix.

____ c. I'd be glad to. Two heads are always better than one.

____ d. Probably, but she's well aware that there's no magic bullet.

____ e. About an hour, once they decided to take a different tack.

C. Use the idioms in your spoken or written answers to the following questions.

1. If there was suddenly no electricity in your home and you needed light, what would *do the trick?*

2. When you have problems with a friend, how do you try to *work* things *out?*

3. What kinds of problems do children sometimes have that could be *nipped in the bud?*

4. Explain how the police would *get to the bottom of* a crime involving murder.

5. What are some illnesses for which there is *no magic bullet?*

D. Using the idioms from this unit or a previous one, tell a classmate about a time when you had a serious problem to solve. You can talk about an imaginary situation. You may want to include the following:

- what the problem was;
- who helped you with it;
- how you approached the problem;
- how long it took you to solve it;
- what the final solution was.

149

Unit 48
Honesty and Secrecy

be on the level   to be honest, to be sincere
also: **be up front**
- The price for that used car was unbelievably low, yet the salesperson claimed that it was in excellent shape. Do you think that he *was on the level?*
- I've never had reason to doubt Cynthia's explanations because she's always *been up front* with me.

level with   to communicate honestly with, to tell the complete truth
also: **give it to someone straight**
USAGE NOTE: These idioms are used when someone suspects that another person is not telling the whole truth, usually out of kindness.
- Please *level with* me. Do you really like my new outfit, or are you just saying you do?
- You're not telling me the whole truth about my chances of winning, are you? I want you to *give it to me straight.*

come clean   to admit the truth about something
- Rather than continue insisting that you didn't do it when everyone knows you did, it's better to *come clean.*
- The criminal's prison term was reduced because she *came clean* and identified her accomplices.

lay one's cards on the table   to present all one's arguments or reasons
- Do you think I'm going to *lay all my cards on the table* to you now? Of course I'm going to save a couple of key arguments for later. See you in court!
- In telephone conversations with the police, the bank robbers holding hostages *laid their cards on the table* and waited for a response.

keep from   to fail to inform
GRAMMAR/USAGE NOTES: This idiom is used with an object. It is used when someone wants to hide knowledge from another person.
- When Barbara won $22 million in the lottery, she *kept* it *from* her friends for a day so that she could recover from the shock.
- Why do you think that I'm not telling the truth? I have nothing to *keep from* you!

skeleton in one's closet   a secret from one's past

GRAMMAR NOTES: *Skeleton* can be made plural. The definite article *the* can be used instead of *one's*.

- Ms. Northrop has decided not to run for the office of vice-mayor because someone has discovered a ***skeleton in her closet.***
- If I told you all my family's ***skeletons in the closet,*** you'd think we were all a strange group.

keep it to oneself   not to reveal a secret
also: **not breathe a word**

- I wanted you to be aware of the situation because you're a friend, but please be sure to ***keep it to yourself*** now that you know.
- Remember, we ca***n't breathe a word*** about what happened. We have to act as if it never occurred.

under the table   in a dishonest and secretive manner

- The attorney gave the corrupt judge a thousand dollars ***under the table*** in order to get the original ruling overturned.
- I wonder how much money is passed ***under the table*** each week by gamblers who never report their winnings as taxable income.

cover up   to attempt to hide the true situation, often an illegal one
related form: **cover-up** (noun)

GRAMMAR NOTE: *Cover up* is separable.

- How could the park commissioner ***cover up*** the illegal payment of salaries to nonexistent employees?
- The inside ***cover-up*** of the murder prevented the police from finding much evidence or identifying any suspects.

white lie   a lie made to avoid embarrassing or insulting someone

USAGE NOTE: The adjectives *small* or *little* are often used.

- When I told my friend that his accent wasn't bad, it was a ***white lie,*** because he really had one of the strongest accents I've ever heard.
- Marie told Franco a small ***white lie*** when she said that she liked his suit. Actually, she thought that it was in very bad taste.

EXERCISES

A. Fill in each blank with the appropriate form of an idiom from this unit. Some sentences may have more than one correct answer.

1. I don't want anyone else to know about my decision yet, so please _____ _____ _____ _____.

2. Mr. Young didn't talk much about his childhood or background, so his colleagues began to think that he had _____ _____ _____ _____.

3. Kaitlin disliked the new furniture in her parents' house, so she had to tell a _____ _____ when they asked for her opinion.

4. If Sharon had _____ _____ her roommate about her new dress, she would have been hurt and disappointed.

5. The politician tried to _____ _____ the fact that he had accepted illegal gifts from constituents in his district.

(continued on next page)

6. The two companies involved in the hostile takeover met in closed session to
_____ _____ _____ _____ _____ _____ and negotiate an
agreement.

7. That real estate deal seems too good to be true. Do you really think that it
_____ _____ _____ _____?

8. Faced with proof of her guilt, the criminal stopped pretending to be innocent
and _____ _____.

9. After conferring with doctors, the family of the terminally ill patient decided to
_____ the bad news _____ him.

10. The mining company made some deals _____ _____ _____ to get
legislation passed to relax environmental standards.

B. **Choose the statement in the right column that best responds to each question in the
left column. Write the appropriate number in the blank.**

1. Should we lay our cards on the
table about the business deal?

2. Was Ann up front with her
boyfriend about his bad breath?

3. What skeleton in the closet has
Mr. Lester been hiding?

4. How was the cover-up of political
bribery finally discovered?

5. Come on, give it to me straight—
Do you really like my new
hairstyle?

____ a. We'd better not. We shouldn't
breathe a word until the deal is final.

____ b. The politician was caught taking
money under the table.

____ c. No, she couldn't level with him about
such a personal matter.

____ d. To be on the level, I'd have to say it
really doesn't fit you.

____ e. He's been keeping from us the fact
that he was once convicted of a
crime.

C. **Use the idioms in your spoken or written answers to the following questions.**

1. Do you agree that sometimes it's necessary to tell a **white lie?** Why or why not? In
what situations?

2. Can you think of anyone famous whose **skeletons in the closet** were recently
revealed by the media? Explain.

3. Do you **keep** your real age **from** other people? Why or why not?

4. If a friend revealed to you that he or she had committed a crime, would you **keep it
to yourself?** Why or why not?

5. What are some situations in which money might be passed **under the table?**

D. **Using the idioms from this unit or a previous one, develop a dialogue or role play in
which the police are questioning a person accused of a crime. You may want to include
the following:**

- the nature of the crime;
- the criminal's attempt to hide the crime;
- how the police try to get the truth from the criminal;
- whether the criminal admits the crime;
- the final outcome.

Unit 49
Danger and Risk

close call   a dangerous situation that could have been worse
also: **close shave**

- Wow, that was a *close call*. I almost stepped out in front of a fast-moving bicycle.
- Before the pilot found an open field in which to make an emergency landing, she had a *close shave* with a tall pine tree.

on the line   in danger, at risk

GRAMMAR/USAGE NOTES: This idiom expresses a condition when used with the verb *be*. It expresses an action when used with the verb *put* and an object.

- A professional boxer must be very well-prepared for each fight because his or her life may be *on the line*.
- The swim coach put it all *on the line* when he guaranteed a winning season to the fund-raising alumni of the school.

touch and go   risky and uncertain

GRAMMAR/USAGE NOTES: This idiom functions as an adjective. It is used when a dangerous situation is capable of developing in more than one direction.

- The rescue of the shipwreck survivors was *touch and go* as a helicopter hovered over the scene and a Coast Guard vessel waited nearby in heavy seas.
- Things were *touch and go* while I tried to find a way out of the worst section of the city I'd ever been in.

take a chance   to be willing to risk something
also: **go out on a limb**

- If those raffle tickets are only a dollar each, I'll *take a chance* with five.
- The politician *went out on a limb* when he predicted that he would easily defeat his opponent.

stick one's neck out   to put oneself in a potentially risky situation
also: **risk one's neck**

USAGE NOTE: The risk is usually to one's job or relationship with others, rather than to one's body.

- The new employee *stuck his neck out* by criticizing company policy at a staff meeting.
- Why should I *risk my neck* for José when he wouldn't do the same for me?

be at stake   to be considered at risk, to be seriously involved

- A lot *is at stake* in the Omega-Turnbull merger. I understand that the combined company would be one of the wealthiest in the chip industry.
- Do you have any idea what's *at stake* in genetic engineering? As a field, it could explode in the coming decades.

play it safe   to be careful, to avoid danger

- The rain is coming down so hard I'm afraid there will be flooding on the roads. We should *play it safe* and stay home.
- Check the fuse box before you attach the microwave oven. It's better to *play it safe* than to be sorry.

out of the woods   no longer in a dangerous situation

- For a while my grandmother was very ill, but then she had a wonderful recovery and now she is completely *out of the woods.*
- The enemy troops could be right behind us, getting ready to attack. Don't relax and think we're *out of the woods* yet.

the chips are down   a situation has reached its most critical or worst point

USAGE NOTE: This idiom often occurs in a *when* clause.

- When *the chips are down,* and you're feeling desperate, remember that no matter what happens, life goes on.
- When the burglar was told that *the chips were down,* he just shrugged and surrendered to police.

EXERCISES

A.   **Fill in each blank with the appropriate form of an idiom from this unit. Some sentences may have more than one correct answer.**

KEN: Hi, Lynn. How did your mother's heart operation go?

LYNN: Not so well. She's not _____ _____ _____ _____ yet.
       $\quad$ 1

KEN: What? Do you mean that her condition is still _____ _____ _____?
      $\quad$ 2

LYNN: Not that serious, but not good either. The heart medication is causing problems

with her liver.

KEN: I'm sorry to hear that. Are the doctors going to _____ _____ _____
      $\quad$ 3

and take her off the medication so that her liver doesn't get damaged?

LYNN: Oh, they can't do that, or her heart may fail. Instead, they're going to _____
       $\quad$ 4

_____ _____ and hope that the effects of the medication on her liver

aren't permanent.

KEN: I see. I guess you have to trust the doctors, because your mom's life _____
      $\quad$ 5

_____ _____.

LYNN: Yes, you're right.

KEN: I don't mean to be flippant, but when _____ _____ _____
      $\quad$ 6

_____, you've got to depend on the doctors. By the way, I heard that you

had a _____ _____ yourself recently while you were jet-skiing.
        7

LYNN: Yeah, my life was _____ _____ _____ there for a while.
                          8

KEN: What happened?

LYNN: I was riding with a friend when he made a sudden turn and a wave caused me

to fall off, and then another jet ski was coming directly toward me!

KEN: Wow, I bet that was scary.

LYNN: It barely missed hitting me. I'll never _____ _____ _____ _____
                                              9

like that again!

B. **Choose the statement in the right column that best responds to each question in the left column. Write the appropriate number in the blank.**

1. Is the boy who almost drowned in the pool out of the woods yet?

2. Why was your job at stake over that business deal?

3. I wonder—Would you put your life on the line for me?

4. Now that you have some money, are you going to play it safe or take a chance and start your own company?

5. We almost stepped in front of a car. That was a close call, wasn't it?

____ a. Are you kidding? I wouldn't risk my neck for anyone!

____ b. Unfortunately, his condition is still touch and go.

____ c. It was. I hope I never have a close shave like that again.

____ d. Because I stuck my neck out and guaranteed the contract.

____ e. I'm going out on a limb, of course. I've always wanted to be my own boss.

C. **Use the idioms in your spoken or written answers to the following questions.**

1. Can you remember a *close call* you had in your life? What was it?

2. If someone was stuck in a burning car and his or her life *was at stake,* would you *stick out your neck* to help? Why or why not?

3. If someone offered you a quick way to get rich by investing your savings, would you put all your money *on the line?* Why or why not?

4. Would you *risk your neck* every day by becoming a police officer? Why do you think some people do?

5. Some people believe that the threat of a nuclear holocaust disappeared with the end of the cold war. Do you think the world is *out of the woods* yet? Why or why not?

D. **Using the idioms from this unit or a previous one, develop a dialogue or role play about two or more people facing a dangerous situation. You may want to include the following:**

- the nature of the situation;
- how serious the situation is;
- how each person reacts in the situation;
- what the outcome is.

155

Unit 50
Beginnings and Endings

come about   to happen

  related idiom: **bring about** (to cause to happen)

  GRAMMAR NOTE: *Come about* is intransitive. *Bring about* is transitive and separable.

  - How did the decision to relocate twenty businesses *come about* without a public hearing?
  - A truck driver who fell asleep on the highway *brought* the accident *about.*

usher in   to begin a distinct age or period of time

  - The 1950s *ushered in* the cold war, a long period of conflict and tension between the forces of democracy and communism.
  - Many people hope that the new century will *usher in* a period of growth and peace in the world.

kick off   to start, to commence

  GRAMMAR NOTE: This idiom is separable.

  - A very talented unknown pianist *kicked off* the show before the virtuoso performance of Gregor Vazhinski.
  - We *kicked* our daughter's birthday party *off* with a magic show.

from scratch   from the beginning

  USAGE NOTES: This idiom is often used when cooking or building something. The verbs *make* or *start* are commonly used.

  - I did not use packaged mashed potatoes. I made everything *from scratch.*
  - The basic frame of the toolshed was wrong, so the carpenter had to start *from scratch.*

turn over a new leaf   to commit to an important change in one's life

  USAGE NOTE: This idiom is used when someone tries to become a better person in action or attitude.

  - On New Year's Eve, some people *turn over a new leaf* by deciding to do things differently in their lives, such as to quit a bad habit.
  - I think that we should take separate vacations this time and really think about our relationship. When we return home, maybe we can *turn over a new leaf.*

bear fruit   to bring good results

- Despite several problems and mistakes, Gene's business efforts *bore fruit* when he received a very large order from the government.
- Seeing one's name in print is a very rewarding way to know that one's efforts have *borne fruit.*

bottom line   the most basic consideration, the most truthful statement

USAGE NOTE: This idiom refers to the most direct cause of a situation, often being greed or self-interest.

- I think you know that the *bottom line* here is profits. If they go down, so do you.
- Look, here's the *bottom line.* I need to borrow your car for an emergency. I promise I'll take care of it, OK?

fall into place   to result in the best possible situation or arrangement
also: **fall together, come together**

- All the different aspects of remodeling our home have finally *fallen into place.* The last of the plumbing has been installed, and we make the last payment tomorrow.
- Isaac was glad that everything *fell together* at the meeting as he had hoped.
- All parts of our plan have *come together.* We can now move on to the next phase.

come out ahead   to benefit more from a situation than to suffer from it
USAGE NOTE: Adverbs such as *way* or *far* can be used.

- If you invest regularly in quality stocks and don't get greedy, stock market history indicates that you'll always *come out ahead.*
- If you make effort to learn your craft when you're young, then you'll be a professional in your prime, and you'll *come out* far *ahead.*

EXERCISES

A.   Fill in each blank with the appropriate form of an idiom from this unit.

1. Harry felt so much better when he _____ _____ _____ _____ _____ and started exercising.

2. I lost my word-processing file before I had a chance to save it. Now I have to start _____ _____ .

3. The mayor _____ _____ the opening ceremony for the bridge by cutting the traditional ribbon with a pair of scissors.

4. The Judds were hopeful that the New Year would _____ _____ a more positive period for their troubled family.

5. Your eye is all black and blue, like you got hit with something. How did it _____ _____ ?

6. I gave the clerk a ten-dollar bill, but she gave me back sixteen dollars and some change. Boy, did I _____ _____ _____ !

7. The production of the big-budget movie seemed hectic and disorganized in the beginning, but eventually everything _____ _____ _____ .

8. At first Josie was concerned that she wouldn't succeed in her studies, but after several months her efforts began to _____ _____ .

B. Choose the statement in the right column that best responds to each question in the left column. Write the appropriate number in the blank.

1. How are you going to usher in the New Year?

2. Is everything in your new business starting to fall into place?

3. How did the controversy over the expenses come about?

4. Does Jenny make all her meals from scratch?

5. Have your real estate investments fallen together yet?

____ a. Maria brought it about when she questioned the costs.

____ b. They're doing OK, but I'm not coming out ahead.

____ c. Once again I'm going to resolve to turn over a new leaf!

____ d. Yes. I'm glad to say that our efforts to start our own company are finally bearing fruit.

____ e. Yes, but the bottom line is that she's not a very good cook.

C. Use the idioms in your spoken or written answers to the following questions.

1. Are your efforts to learn English starting to *bear fruit?* How?

2. Tell or write about an important decision you have made. How did the decision *come about?*

3. What foods can you (or someone you know) make *from scratch?*

4. Have you ever promised to *turn over a new leaf?* Explain.

5. How do you *usher in* the New Year?

D. Using the idioms from this unit or a previous one, develop a dialogue or role play about friends discussing the New Year. You may want to include the following:

- how they're going to celebrate New Year's Eve;
- when their celebration starts;
- what changes they've promised to make in their lives;
- how the future looks for each of them.

Review:Units 41–50

A. Circle the expression that best completes each sentence.

1. I know someone called Jeff Larsen, but the name Jack Larsen doesn't _____.
   a. ring a bell
   b. beat my brains
   c. catch my eye

2. Anthony is certain that all the long hours of writing will _____ when his first novel is published.
   a. bear fruit
   b. come clean
   c. iron out

3. The little girl tried to _____ the fact that she had gone to a friend's house after school instead of coming home.
   a. settle on
   b. cover up
   c. think over

4. Jaime traveled extensively while he was in the United States in order to _____.
   a. have a way with words
   b. go out on a limb
   c. broaden his horizons

5. Could you please tell me what time the concert _____?
   a. gets underway
   b. ushers in
   c. comes together

6. At first Lenora thought that she had made the right decision, but later, she _____ about the purchase.
   a. took into account
   b. had second thoughts
   c. jumped to conclusions

7. I'm trying to talk on the telephone. Could you please _____?
   a. blurt out
   b. hold it down
   c. fire away

8. Kevin wasn't too hungry, so a banana .
   a. did the trick
   b. took his pick
   c. was food for thought

9. Building more jails is _____ for the crime problem. We've got to attack the root causes in society that lead to crime.
   a. cover-up
   b. pie in the sky
   c. no magic bullet

10. When the company started losing money, the directors fired the management team and _____ themselves.
    a. fell together
    b. called the shots
    c. stood out

B. Indicate whether each statement is TRUE (T) or FALSE (F).

_____ 1. If you're going back and forth on a decision, then you've already made up your mind.
_____ 2. One way of leveling with someone is to lay your cards on the table.
_____ 3. You might tell a white lie if you were beating around the bush.
_____ 4. When the chips are down, someone might negotiate under the table as a last resort.
_____ 5. If you have to wrack your brains to find a solution, it dawns on you right away.
_____ 6. You'd be more likely to turn over a new leaf when your future is at stake.
_____ 7. Someone who has a hare-brained scheme has considered the pros and cons carefully.
_____ 8. The importance of a situation might sink in if you gave it some thought.
_____ 9. If you want to play it safe, you shouldn't stick your neck out.
_____ 10. If you heard something through the grapevine, then you'd definitely be out of the loop.

159

C. Complete the puzzle with the missing parts of the idioms in the sentences below.

ACROSS

2. It goes without ____ that money talks.
5. Deirdre made the cake from _____ .
7. Cindy has the _____-how to fix the plumbing.
9. That lonely man must have a ____ in the closet.
12. I solved the problem by putting two and two _____ .
14. This is a waste of time. Let's take a ____ tack.
16. What's the matter—cat got your _____ ?
17. How did the conflict with your boss come ____ ?

DOWN

1. His birthday never crossed my _____ .
3. Did Aaron's decision take everything into ____ ?
4. It's better to play it ____ than to be sorry.
6. That falling branch was a ____ call, wasn't it?
8. Please pay _____ to what the teacher is saying.
9. Jack can't decide now. He needs to ____ on it.
10. Is Rick on the ____ when he says he'll do it?
11. The badly injured patient is out of the ____ now.
13. I'm not going to risk my ____ by skydiving.
15. Eight words per line is a general rule of _____ .

160

Index

Index

Answer Key

Unit 1

Exercise A
1. As soon as
2. right away/at once
3. miss a beat
4. at the last minute
5. was just about to
6. So far
7. all of a sudden
8. in the long run
9. in no time/in a flash

Exercise B
a. 2 b. 4 c. 1 d. 3 e. 5

Unit 2

Exercise A
1. all told
2. piled up
3. at least
4. a number of/a lot of
5. the lion's share
6. or so
7. come up short
8. a drop in the bucket
9. are left

Exercise B
a. 3 b. 1 c. 2 d. 5 e. 4

Unit 3

Exercise A
1. collecting dust
2. turn out
3. cranked out/whipped out
4. made to order
5. cut down on/cut back on
6. pack rat
7. ran out of
8. brings out
9. go through/use up

Exercise B
a. 2 b. 5 c. 3 d. 1 e. 4

Unit 4

Exercise A
1. in a hurry/in a rush
2. at a snail's pace
3. hurry up
4. on the double
5. slowed down/ slowed up
6. inching along
7. picked up

Exercise B
a. 3 b. 1 c. 2 d. 5 e. 4

Unit 5

Exercise A
1. am wound up

2. took her own sweet time
3. Hold your horses
4. try my patience
5. on pins and needles
6. sit tight
7. jumped the gun
8. on edge

Exercise B
a. 5 b. 1 c. 2 d. 3 e. 4

Unit 6

Exercise A
1. do over
2. goof up/slip up
3. messed up
4. mixed up
5. think straight
6. put my foot in my mouth
7. on the wrong track
8. slip of the tongue
9. got our wires crossed/
   got our signals crossed

Exercise B
a. 3 b. 2 c. 5 d. 1 e. 4

Unit 7

Exercise A
1. play it by ear
2. map out/chart out
3. on the spur of the moment
4. is in the works
5. draw up
6. cooked up
7. ruled out
8. is up in the air

Exercise B
a. 1 b. 5 c. 2 d. 4 e. 3

Unit 8

Exercise A
1. long shot
2. pipe dream
3. irons in the fire
4. missed the boat
5. passed up
6. stand a chance
7. miss out on
8. chances are that/odds are that
9. put all your eggs in one basket
10. is iffy

Exercise B
a. 2 b. 3 c. 1 d. 5 e. 4

Unit 9

Exercise A
1. do a favor
2. real sport
3. bent over backwards

4. take turns
5. play ball with
6. pulled together
7. it takes two to tango
8. put our heads together

Exercise B
a. 5 b. 3 c. 1 d. 2 e. 4

Unit 10

Exercise A
1. wishful thinking
2. Break a leg
3. held out hope
4. lucked out
5. the sky's the limit
6. hope for the best
7. not the end of the world
8. every cloud has a silver lining
9. are looking up
10. keep our fingers crossed

Exercise B
a. 2 b. 1 c. 5 d. 3 e. 4

Review: Units 1–10

Exercise A
1. a 2. a 3. c 4. a 5. b
6. a 7. c 8. c 9. b 10. b

Exercise B
1. T 2. F 3. T 4. F 5. T
6. T 7. F 8. T 9. T 10. T

Exercise C

ACROSS	DOWN
2. cook	1. chance
3. favor	2. cloud
5. basket	4. away
11. sudden	6. together
12. slow	7. fingers
13. moment	8. least
15. patience	9. number
16. horses	10. mouth
	14. tango

Unit 11

Exercise A
1. face to face
2. tied the knot
3. hit it off
4. get along with
5. rub elbows with
6. make friends
7. on the rocks
8. started off on the wrong foot

Exercise B
a. 4 b. 2 c. 1 d. 5 e. 3

Unit 12

Exercise A
1. has a good head on her shoulders
2. live wire
3. hot-headed
4. soft-hearted
5. was out of character
6. thick-skinned
7. soft in the head
8. tough cookie
9. stick in the mud/bump on a log

Exercise B
a. 3   b. 1   c. 4   d. 2   e. 5

Unit 13

Exercise A
1. creature comforts of home
2. on the go/on the run
3. running around in circles
4. rat race
5. dog-eat-dog world
6. keep up with the Joneses
7. in a rut
8. couch potato
9. back to the same old grind

Exercise B
a. 3   b. 1   c. 5   d. 2   e. 4

Unit 14

Exercise A
1. stop and go
2. bumper-to-bumper
3. U-turn
4. as far as
5. turn around
6. fender bender
7. pull over
8. wrapped up
9. pull into/turn into
10. up to speed

Exercise B
a. 4   b. 5   c. 2   d. 3   e. 1

Unit 15

Exercise A
1. bounced a check
2. made out
3. on credit
4. take out
5. paid off
6. put aside/lay aside/set aside
7. pay back
8. two bits
9. chip in

Exercise B
a. 3   b. 5   c. 1   d. 2   e. 4

Unit 16

Exercise A
1. household word/ household name
2. set up shop
3. on the market
4. doing business
5. lay off
6. rank-and-file
7. going out of business
8. went on strike
9. head-hunter
10. put in for

Exercise B
a. 5   b. 3   c. 2   d. 1   e. 4

Unit 17

Exercise A
1. middle-of-the-road
2. take office
3. sound bite
4. party line
5. red tape
6. grass-roots
7. run for office
8. press the flesh

Exercise B
a. 2   b. 3   c. 1   d. 5   e. 4

Unit 18

Exercise A
1. loose cannon
2. play favorites
3. run the show
4. in hand
5. runs a tight ship
6. asleep at the wheel
7. throw his weight around
8. pull some strings
9. be on the take

Exercise B
a. 4   b. 1   c. 3   d. 2   e. 5

Unit 19

Exercise A
1. enter into
2. go-between
3. cut a deal
4. meet halfway
5. are on the table
6. happy medium
7. drive a hard bargain
8. give and take
9. break off

Exercise B
a. 2   b. 3   c. 4   d. 1   e. 5

Unit 20

Exercise A
1. Cross my heart

2. followed through
3. Famous last words
4. given his word
5. lived up to
6. came through for
7. keeps her word
8. stick to

Exercise B
a. 2   b. 1   c. 5   d. 3   e. 4

Review: Units 11–20

Exercise A
1. b   2. a   3. c   4. b   5. a
6. c   7. a   8. b   9. a   10. c

Exercise B
1. T   2. F   3. T   4. F   5. T
6. F   7. F   8. F   9. T   10. T

Exercise C

Across	Down
1. strike	1. speed
3. check	2. business
5. medium	4. character
8. office	6. between
9. grindstone	7. cannon
12. middle	10. bits
14. face	11. world
15. shoulders	13. promise
18. Famous	16. soft
19. creature	17. hand

Unit 21

Exercise A
1. break out in/into tears; burst out in/into tears
2. broke my heart/burst my bubble
3. get to
4. burst my bubble/break my heart
5. hard pill to swallow
6. open up
7. choked up
8. got off my chest
9. pour out
10. is music to my ears

Exercise B
a. 5   b. 1   c. 2   d. 3   e. 4

Unit 22

Exercise A
1. pumped up/fired up
2. liven up
3. might as well
4. not give a damn/not give a hoot
5. throw cold water on
6. it's all the same to
7. get into the spirit
8. are crazy about/are nuts about
9. going with the crowd

Answer Key

Exercise B
a. 2   b. 4   c. 1   d. 5   e. 3

Unit 23

Exercise A
1. What on earth/What the devil
2. gave me a start
3. threw for a loop
4. heart-stopper
5. drop a bombshell
6. turn over in her grave
7. took by surprise
8. taken aback

Exercise B
a. 1   b. 5   c. 4   d. 3   e. 2

Unit 24

Exercise A
1. for laughs
2. tickles my funny bone
3. meant business
4. hit home
5. no laughing matter
6. keep a straight face
7. doubled up
8. liven up
9. cracked up

Exercise B
a. 5   b. 3   c. 2   d. 1   e. 4

Unit 25

Exercise A
1. save face
2. have a heart
3. red-faced
4. on the spot
5. a shoulder to cry on
6. My heart goes out to
7. feel sorry for/take pity on
8. my ears were burning
9. live down

Exercise B
a. 2   b. 3   c. 1   d. 5   e. 4

Unit 26

Exercise A
1. take pride in
2. his pride and joy
3. was stuck up
4. stole the show
5. blow my own horn/toot my own horn
6. hurt my feelings
7. taken a back seat to
8. hold your head high/keep your chin up

Exercise B
a. 4   b. 1   c. 2   d. 3   e. 5

Unit 27

Exercise A
1. caused a stir
2. blow the whistle
3. rocked the boat
4. harping on
5. making a big deal of/making a big deal about
6. ranting and raving
7. had words with
8. have it out with
9. have an ax to grind
10. splitting hairs

Exercise B
a. 1   b. 3   c. 4   d. 5   e. 2

Unit 28

Exercise A
1. broken record
2. eating at
3. thorn in the side/fly in the ointment
4. pet peeves
5. hit a nerve
6. ruffled some feathers
7. get on my nerves
8. rub the wrong way
9. getting into my hair

Exercise B
a. 2   b. 4   c. 5   d. 1   e. 3

Unit 29

Exercise A
1. kick myself for
2. raise eyebrows
3. weighing on my mind
4. is too bad
5. losing sleep over
6. make much of
7. come back to haunt
8. not give a thought

Exercise B
a. 3   b. 1   c. 5   d. 2   e. 4

Unit 30

Exercise A
1. the last straw
2. put up with/grin and bear
3. at the end of my rope
4. fed up with
5. beating your head against the wall
6. drew the line at
7. pulling your hair out over
8. put an end to

Exercise B
a. 5   b. 3   c. 1   d. 2   e. 4

Review: Units 21–30

Exercise A
1. c   2. a   3. b   4. c   5. a
6. b   7. c   8. a   9. a   10. b

Exercise B
1. F   2. T   3. F   4. T   5. T
6. F   7. F   8. T   9. T   10. F

Exercise C

ACROSS	DOWN
2. pity	1. line
3. laughs	3. Lighten
6. rave	4. hairs
7. world	5. bone
10. surprise	8. laughing
11. eat	9. might
13. blanket	11. eyebrows
15. chin	12. rope
16. peeve	13. boat
17. ointment	14. apple
18. nest	

Unit 31

Exercise A
1. saw eye to eye
2. on the same wavelength
3. You can say that again.
4. war of words
5. were at odds with
6. go along
7. are for
8. sided with

Exercise B
a. 5   b. 3   c. 1   d. 2   e. 4

Unit 32

Exercise A
1. look after
2. carry her weight
3. see to/see about
4. leave to
5. dumped on
6. take on
7. carry the ball
8. take over
9. see through/carry through

Exercise B
a. 2   b. 3   c. 4   d. 1   e. 5

Unit 33

Exercise A
1. paper trail
2. jump on the bandwagon
3. acid test
4. stood behind
5. not have a leg to stand on
6. pulled for
7. bear out
8. back up
9. came out for
10. stood up for

Exercise B
a. 1   b. 3   c. 2   d. 5   e. 4

Unit 34

Exercise A
1. speak to
2. words of wisdom
3. took under her wing
4. pitch in
5. turn to/look to
6. bum steer
7. steer straight
8. sound out
9. lending me a hand

Exercise B
a. 3   b. 1   c. 2   d. 5   e. 4

Unit 35

Exercise A
1. on his second wind
2. coming on strong
3. stepped up
4. get after/keep after
5. follow up on
6. giving it her best shot
7. go overboard

Exercise B
a. 2   b. 3   c. 5   d. 1   e. 4

Unit 36

Exercise A
1. made headway
2. keep up
3. on a roll
4. fallen behind
5. catch up with
6. gained steam
7. under way
8. take shape
9. coming along/going along
10. So far, so good

Exercise B
a. 2   b. 3   c. 1   d. 4   e. 5

Unit 37

Exercise A
1. shot in the arm
2. pep talk
3. talked up
4. hang in there
5. cheered on
6. bring around to
7. talk into
8. give in to

Exercise B
a. 2   b. 4   c. 3   d. 1   e. 5

Unit 38

Exercise A
1. gets her way/has her way

2. take a stand
3. stood his ground
4. put my foot down
5. stubborn as a mule
6. set her sights on
7. went to great lengths
8. bent on

Exercise B
a. 2   b. 3   c. 1   d. 5   e. 4

Unit 39

Exercise A
1. Nice going
2. owe you one
3. hand it to
4. owe it to
5. Thanks to
6. thanked her lucky stars/ counted her lucky stars
7. pat myself on the back
8. tipped his hat to

Exercise B
a. 4   b. 1   c. 2   d. 5   e. 3

Unit 40

Exercise A
1. fit the bill
2. go for
3. grow on
4. turns my stomach
5. be in the mood for
6. for the birds
7. could care less for/ couldn't care less for
8. made my skin crawl/ gave me the creeps

Exercise B
a. 5   b. 1   c. 2   d. 3   e. 4

Review: Units 31–40

Exercise A
1. b   2. a   3. c   4. a   5. c
6. a   7. b   8. c   9. a   10. b

Exercise B
1. T   2. F   3. T   4. F   5. F
6. T   7. T   8. T   9. F   10. T

Exercise C

ACROSS	DOWN
1. take	2. around
7. speak	3. less
8. backup	4. guns
9. Thanks	5. paper
10. weight	6. cheer
11. creeps	8. behind
14. odds	12. pig
17. wing	13. going
18. shot	15. stars
	16. follow
	17. way

Unit 41

Exercise A
1. broaden his horizons
2. heard of
3. picked up
4. make of
5. know-how
6. got wind of
7. was news to
8. through the grapevine
9. in the loop

Exercise B
a. 3   b. 5   c. 1   d. 2   e. 4

Unit 42

Exercise A
1. having second thoughts
2. going back and forth
3. take back
4. food for thought
5. think over
6. sleep on it
7. think through
8. take into consideration/take into account

Exercise B
a. 2   b. 5   c. 1   d. 4   e. 3

Unit 43

Exercise A
1. rings a bell
2. stands out/sticks out
3. pay attention to
4. dawned on/occurred to
5. took note of
6. caught her eye
7. look out for
8. sink in

Exercise B
a. 2   b. 1   c. 5   d. 3   e. 4

Unit 44

Exercise A
1. no rhyme or reason/ neither rhyme nor reason
2. putting the cart before the horse
3. pie in the sky
4. hare-brained
5. jump to conclusions
6. put two and two together
7. goes without saying/stands to reason
8. stands to reason/ goes without saying

Exercise B
a. 2   b. 1   c. 4   d. 3   e. 5

Answer Key

Unit 45

Exercise A
1. hold down
2. blurted out
3. the cat have your tongue
4. speak her mind
5. fire away
6. has a way with words/has a gift for gab
7. shut up
8. clammed up
9. beat around the bush

Exercise B
a. 5   b. 3   c. 1   d. 2   e. 4

Unit 46

Exercise A
1. leave up to
2. make up my mind
3. take your pick
4. take it or leave it
5. pros and cons
6. calls the shots
7. leave open
8. settled on
9. rule of thumb

Exercise B
a. 4   b. 1   c. 5   d. 2   e. 3

Unit 47

Exercise A
1. as a last resort
2. quick fix
3. take a different tack
4. wracked her brains/beat her brains
5. two heads are better than one
6. nip in the bud
7. do the trick
8. no magic bullet
9. get to the bottom of
10. work out/iron out

Exercise B
a. 3   b. 5   c. 1   d. 2   e. 4

Unit 48

Exercise A
1. keep it to yourself/ don't breathe a word
2. skeletons in his closet
3. white lie
4. leveled with
5. cover up
6. lay their cards on the table
7. is on the level
8. came clean
9. keep from
10. under the table

Exercise B
a. 1   b. 4   c. 2   d. 5   e. 3

Unit 49

Exercise A
1. out of the woods
2. touch and go
3. play it safe/take a chance
4. take a chance/play it safe
5. is at stake
6. the chips are down
7. close call
8. on the line
9. stick my neck out

Exercise B
a. 3   b. 1   c. 5   d. 2   e. 4

UNIT 50

Exercise A
1. turned over a new leaf
2. from scratch
3. kicked off
4. usher in
5. come about
6. come out ahead
7. fell into place
8. bear fruit

Exercise B
a. 3   b. 5   c. 1   d. 2   e. 4

Review: Units 41–50

Exercise A
1. a   2. a   3. b   4. c   5. a
6. b   7. b   8. a   9. c   10. b

Exercise B
1. F   2. T   3. T   4. T   5. F
6. T   7. F   8. T   9. T   10. F

Exercise C

Across	Down
2. saying	1. mind
5. scratch	3. account
7. know	4. safe
9. skeleton	6. close
12. together	8. attention
14. different	9. sleep
16. tongue	10. level
17. about	11. woods
	13. neck
	15. thumb